GEORGE WASHINGTON

GEORGE WASHINGTON

Roger Bruns

Director of Publications
National Historical Publications and Records Commission
Washington, D.C.

CHELSEA HOUSE PUBLISHERS
NEW YORK
PHILADELPHIA

EDITORIAL DIRECTOR: Nancy Toff
SENIOR EDITOR: John W. Selfridge
ASSOCIATE EDITOR: Marian W. Taylor
MANAGING EDITOR: Karyn Gullen Browne
COPY CHIEF: Perry King
EDITORIAL STAFF: Maria Behan, Karen Dreste,
            Pierre Hauser, Kathleen McDermott,
            Howard Ratner, Alma Rodriguez-Sokol,
            Bert Yaeger
PICTURE EDITOR: Elizabeth Terhune
PICTURE RESEARCH: Ian Ensign
ART DIRECTOR: Giannella Garrett
LAYOUT: Irene Friedman
ART ASSISTANTS: Noreen Lamb, Carol McDougall,
            Victoria Tomaselli
COVER ILLUSTRATION: Frank Steiner

Frontispiece courtesy of The Bettmann Archive

3 5 7 9 8 6 4 2

Library of Congress Cataloging in Publication Data

Bruns, Roger. GEORGE WASHINGTON.
(World leaders past & present)
Bibliography: p.
Includes index.
1. Washington, George, 1732–1799—Juvenile literature.
2. Presidents—United States—Biography—Juvenile
literature. I. Title. II. Series.
E312.66.B74   1986   973.4′1′0924 [B]   86-21595

ISBN 0-87754-584-7
    0-7910-0668-9 (pbk.)

Contents

WORLD LEADERS   PAST & PRESENT

John Adams
John Quincy Adams
Konrad Adenauer
Alexander the Great
Salvador Allende
Marc Antony
Corazon Aquino
Yasir Arafat
King Arthur
Hafez al-Assad
Kemal Atatürk
Attila
Clement Attlee
Augustus Caesar
Menachem Begin
David Ben-Gurion
Otto von Bismarck
Léon Blum
Simon Bolívar
Cesare Borgia
Willy Brandt
Leonid Brezhnev
Julius Caesar
John Calvin
Jimmy Carter
Fidel Castro
Catherine the Great
Charlemagne
Chiang Kai-Shek
Winston Churchill
Georges Clemenceau
Cleopatra
Constantine the Great
Hernán Cortés
Oliver Cromwell
Georges-Jacques
 Danton
Jefferson Davis
Moshe Dayan
Charles de Gaulle
Eamon De Valera
Eugene Debs
Deng Xiaoping
Benjamin Disraeli
Alexander Dubček
François & Jean-Claude
 Duvalier
Dwight Eisenhower
Eleanor of Aquitaine
Elizabeth i
Faisal
Ferdinand & Isabella
Francisco Franco
Benjamin Franklin

Frederick the Great
Indira Gandhi
Mohandas Gandhi
Giuseppe Garibaldi
Amin & Bashir Gemayel
Genghis Khan
William Gladstone
Mikhail Gorbachev
Ulysses S. Grant
Ernesto "Che" Guevara
Tenzin Gyatso
Alexander Hamilton
Dag Hammarskjöld
Henry viii
Henry of Navarre
Paul von Hindenburg
Hirohito
Adolf Hitler
Ho Chi Minh
King Hussein
Ivan the Terrible
Andrew Jackson
James i
Wojciech Jaruzelski
Thomas Jefferson
Joan of Arc
Pope John xxiii
Pope John Paul ii
Lyndon Johnson
Benito Juárez
John Kennedy
Robert Kennedy
Jomo Kenyatta
Ayatollah Khomeini
Nikita Khrushchev
Kim Il Sung
Martin Luther King, Jr.
Henry Kissinger
Kublai Khan
Lafayette
Robert E. Lee
Vladimir Lenin
Abraham Lincoln
David Lloyd George
Louis xiv
Martin Luther
Judas Maccabeus
James Madison
Nelson & Winnie
 Mandela
Mao Zedong
Ferdinand Marcos
George Marshall

Mary, Queen of Scots
Tomáš Masaryk
Golda Meir
Klemens von Metternich
James Monroe
Hosni Mubarak
Robert Mugabe
Benito Mussolini
Napoléon Bonaparte
Gamal Abdel Nasser
Jawaharlal Nehru
Nero
Nicholas II
Richard Nixon
Kwame Nkrumah
Daniel Ortega
Mohammed Reza Pahlavi
Thomas Paine
Charles Stewart
 Parnell
Pericles
Juan Perón
Peter the Great
Pol Pot
Muammar el-Qaddafi
Ronald Reagan
Cardinal Richelieu
Maximilien Robespierre
Eleanor Roosevelt
Franklin Roosevelt
Theodore Roosevelt
Anwar Sadat
Haile Selassie
Prince Sihanouk
Jan Smuts
Joseph Stalin
Sukarno
Sun Yat-sen
Tamerlane
Mother Teresa
Margaret Thatcher
Josip Broz Tito
Toussaint L'Ouverture
Leon Trotsky
Pierre Trudeau
Harry Truman
Queen Victoria
Lech Walesa
George Washington
Chaim Weizmann
Woodrow Wilson
Xerxes
Emiliano Zapata
Zhou Enlai

CHELSEA HOUSE PUBLISHERS

ON LEADERSHIP
Arthur M. Schlesinger, jr.

LEADERSHIP, it may be said, is really what makes the world go round. Love no doubt smooths the passage; but love is a private transaction between consenting adults. Leadership is a public transaction with history. The idea of leadership affirms the capacity of individuals to move, inspire, and mobilize masses of people so that they act together in pursuit of an end. Sometimes leadership serves good purposes, sometimes bad; but whether the end is benign or evil, great leaders are those men and women who leave their personal stamp on history.

Now, the very concept of leadership implies the proposition that individuals can make a difference. This proposition has never been universally accepted. From classical times to the present day, eminent thinkers have regarded individuals as no more than the agents and pawns of larger forces, whether the gods and goddesses of the ancient world or, in the modern era, race, class, nation, the dialectic, the will of the people, the spirit of the times, history itself. Against such forces, the individual dwindles into insignificance.

So contends the thesis of historical determinism. Tolstoy's great novel *War and Peace* offers a famous statement of the case. Why, Tolstoy asked, did millions of men in the Napoleonic wars, denying their human feelings and their common sense, move back and forth across Europe slaughtering their fellows? "The war," Tolstoy answered, "was bound to happen simply because it was bound to happen." All prior history predetermined it. As for leaders, they, Tolstoy said, "are but the labels that serve to give a name to an end and, like labels, they have the least possible connection with the event." The greater the leader, "the more conspicuous the inevitability and the predestination of every act he commits." The leader, said Tolstoy, is "the slave of history."

Determinism takes many forms. Marxism is the determinism of class. Nazism the determinism of race. But the idea of men and women as the slaves of history runs athwart the deepest human instincts. Rigid determinism abolishes the idea of human freedom—

the assumption of free choice that underlies every move we make, every word we speak, every thought we think. It abolishes the idea of human responsibility, since it is manifestly unfair to reward or punish people for actions that are by definition beyond their control. No one can live consistently by any deterministic creed. The Marxist states prove this themselves by their extreme susceptibility to the cult of leadership.

More than that, history refutes the idea that individuals make no difference. In December 1931 a British politician crossing Park Avenue in New York City between 76th and 77th Streets around 10:30 P.M. looked in the wrong direction and was knocked down by an automobile—a moment, he later recalled, of a man aghast, a world aglare: "I do not understand why I was not broken like an eggshell or squashed like a gooseberry." Fourteen months later an American politician, sitting in an open car in Miami, Florida, was fired on by an assassin; the man beside him was hit. Those who believe that individuals make no difference to history might well ponder whether the next two decades would have been the same had Mario Constasino's car killed Winston Churchill in 1931 and Giuseppe Zangara's bullet killed Franklin Roosevelt in 1933. Suppose, in addition, that Adolf Hitler had been killed in the street fighting during the Munich *Putsch* of 1923 and that Lenin had died of typhus during World War I. What would the 20th century be like now?

For better or for worse, individuals do make a difference. "The notion that a people can run itself and its affairs anonymously," wrote the philosopher William James, "is now well known to be the silliest of absurdities. Mankind does nothing save through initiatives on the part of inventors, great or small, and imitation by the rest of us—these are the sole factors in human progress. Individuals of genius show the way, and set the patterns, which common people then adopt and follow."

Leadership, James suggests, means leadership in thought as well as in action. In the long run, leaders in thought may well make the greater difference to the world. But, as Woodrow Wilson once said, "Those only are leaders of men, in the general eye, who lead in action. . . . It is at their hands that new thought gets its translation into the crude language of deeds." Leaders in thought often invent in solitude and obscurity, leaving to later generations the tasks of imitation. Leaders in action—the leaders portrayed in this series—have to be effective in their own time.

And they cannot be effective by themselves. They must act in response to the rhythms of their age. Their genius must be adapted, in a phrase of William James's, "to the receptivities of the moment." Leaders are useless without followers. "There goes the mob," said the French politician hearing a clamor in the streets. "I am their leader. I must follow them." Great leaders turn the inchoate emotions of the mob to purposes of their own. They seize on the opportunities of their time, the hopes, fears, frustrations, crises, potentialities. They succeed when events have prepared the way for them, when the community is awaiting to be aroused, when they can provide the clarifying and organizing ideas. Leadership ignites the circuit between the individual and the mass and thereby alters history.

It may alter history for better or for worse. Leaders have been responsible for the most extravagant follies and most monstrous crimes that have beset suffering humanity. They have also been vital in such gains as humanity has made in individual freedom, religious and racial tolerance, social justice and respect for human rights.

There is no sure way to tell in advance who is going to lead for good and who for evil. But a glance at the gallery of men and women in *World Leaders—Past and Present* suggests some useful tests.

One test is this: do leaders lead by force or by persuasion? By command or by consent? Through most of history leadership was exercised by the divine right of authority. The duty of followers was to defer and to obey. "Theirs not to reason why,/ Theirs but to do and die." On occasion, as with the so-called "enlightened despots" of the 18th century in Europe, absolutist leadership was animated by humane purposes. More often, absolutism nourished the passion for domination, land, gold and conquest and resulted in tyranny.

The great revolution of modern times has been the revolution of equality. The idea that all people should be equal in their legal condition has undermined the old structure of authority, hierarchy and deference. The revolution of equality has had two contrary effects on the nature of leadership. For equality, as Alexis de Tocqueville pointed out in his great study *Democracy in America,* might mean equality in servitude as well as equality in freedom.

"I know of only two methods of establishing equality in the political world," Tocqueville wrote. "Rights must be given to every citizen, or none at all to anyone . . . save one, who is the master of all." There was no middle ground "between the sovereignty of all and the absolute power of one man." In his astonishing prediction of 20th-century totalitarian dictatorship, Tocqueville explained how the revolution of equality could lead to the *"Führerprinzip"* and more terrible absolutism than the world had ever known.

But when rights are given to every citizen and the sovereignty of all is established, the problem of leadership takes a new form, becomes more exacting than ever before. It is easy to issue commands and enforce them by the rope and the stake, the concentration camp and the *gulag.* It is much harder to use argument and achievement to overcome opposition and win consent. The Founding Fathers of the United States understood the difficulty. They believed that history had given them the opportunity to decide, as Alexander Hamilton wrote in the first Federalist Paper, whether men are indeed capable of basing government on "reflection and choice, or whether they are forever destined to depend . . . on accident and force."

Government by reflection and choice called for a new style of leadership and a new quality of followership. It required leaders to be responsive to popular concerns, and it required followers to be active and informed participants in the process. Democracy does not eliminate emotion from politics; sometimes it fosters demagoguery; but it is confident that, as the greatest of democratic leaders put it, you cannot fool all of the people all of the time. It measures leadership by results and retires those who overreach or falter or fail.

It is true that in the long run despots are measured by results too. But they can postpone the day of judgment, sometimes indefinitely, and in the meantime they can do infinite harm. It is also true that democracy is no guarantee of virtue and intelligence in government, for the voice of the people is not necessarily the voice of God. But democracy, by assuring the right of opposition, offers built-in resistance to the evils inherent in absolutism. As the theologian Reinhold Niebuhr summed it up, "Man's capacity for justice makes democracy possible, but man's inclination to injustice makes democracy necessary."

A second test for leadership is the end for which power is sought. When leaders have as their goal the supremacy of a master race or the promotion of totalitarian revolution or the acquisition and exploitation of colonies or the protection of greed and privilege or the preservation of personal power, it is likely that their leadership will do little to advance the cause of humanity. When their goal is the abolition of slavery, the liberation of women, the enlargement of opportunity for the poor and powerless, the extension of equal rights to racial minorities, the defense of the freedoms of expression and opposition, it is likely that their leadership will increase the sum of human liberty and welfare.

Leaders have done great harm to the world. They have also conferred great benefits. You will find both sorts in this series. Even "good" leaders must be regarded with a certain wariness. Leaders are not demigods; they put on their trousers one leg after another just like ordinary mortals. No leader is infallible, and every leader needs to be reminded of this at regular intervals. Irreverence irritates leaders but is their salvation. Unquestioning submission corrupts leaders and demands followers. Making a cult of a leader is always a mistake. Fortunately hero worship generates its own antidote. "Every hero," said Emerson, "becomes a bore at last."

The signal benefit the great leaders confer is to embolden the rest of us to live according to our own best selves, to be active, insistent, and resolute in affirming our own sense of things. For great leaders attest to the reality of human freedom against the supposed inevitabilities of history. And they attest to the wisdom and power that may lie within the most unlikely of us, which is why Abraham Lincoln remains the supreme example of great leadership. A great leader, said Emerson, exhibits new possibilities to all humanity. "We feed on genius. . . . Great men exist that there may be greater men."

Great leaders, in short, justify themselves by emancipating and empowering their followers. So humanity struggles to master its destiny, remembering with Alexis de Tocqueville: "It is true that around every man a fatal circle is traced beyond which he cannot pass; but within the wide verge of that circle he is powerful and free; as it is with man, so with communities."

—*New York*

1

Inauguration

New York City, April 30, 1789 — From the southern end of Manhattan Island, a 13-gun salute greets the sunrise. At Number 3 Cherry Street, a tall, dignified man powders his hair, dresses in a suit of brown broadcloth, white silk stockings, and shoes with silver buckles. Hanging at his side is an elegant sword.

Church bells begin to toll, crowds to gather, militia companies to form ranks. At noon, a grand coach drawn by four horses pulls in front of the house, preceded by lines of troops and carriages filled with officials. As cheering bystanders strain to catch sight of him, the tall man strides from the house and enters the carriage. The procession rolls slowly toward Federal Hall, the seat of the national Congress. Along the route, thousands of New Yorkers and visitors from the other 12 American states wave and shout, wildly excited by the presence of the man to whom they have for so long entrusted their fate, and to whom they have again turned for national leadership. America is saluting General George Washington.

Behind Washington now were the years of uncer-

He is the purest figure in history.
—WILLIAM EWART GLADSTONE
19th-century British
politician, on Washington

George Washington (1732–1799) was the subject of innumerable paintings, both during his lifetime and after it. This portrait first appeared in Washington Irving's 1855 biography, *Life of Washington*. A namesake of the first U.S. president, Irving also wrote "Rip Van Winkle" and "The Legend of Sleepy Hollow."

Number 3 Cherry Street, the Manhattan house where Washington lived during the first year of his presidency. In 1790 the federal government moved from New York to Philadelphia; 10 years later it was permanently established in Washington, D.C., the new city named for the nation's first president.

The preservation of the sacred fire of liberty and the destiny of the republican model of government are justly considered as deeply, perhaps as finally staked upon the experiment entrusted to the hands of the American people.
—GEORGE WASHINGTON
from his inaugural address

tainty, both about his own destiny and that of his countrymen. Together they had challenged the rule of the British in America, fought a long and painful war of revolution, survived the bleak days when victory seemed impossible. Washington had written then, "our present situation . . . is beyond description, irksome, and dangerous." He had grieved over the condition of his "wretched remains of a broken army" and feared that "the game is pretty near up."

But Washington and his fellow Americans had faced and conquered starvation and disease; they had challenged a mighty, well-seasoned army and prevailed. Many had paid for the victory with their lives, but they had produced a new nation, free and independent. To govern that nation, America's leaders had written a Constitution. One of the provisions of this document called for a national chief executive — a president — of the United States.

On this sunny April day in New York, George Washington prepares to accept that position. The inaugural procession stops at Federal Hall, where both houses of the Congress await the historic ceremony. As Washington enters, the lawmakers and guests rise.

Led by another eminent figure of the American

Revolution, John Adams, Washington steps onto a balcony overlooking Wall Street. From crowded rooftops, from windows in surrounding buildings, from the packed streets below, an enormous ovation erupts. Washington bows, his hand on his heart.

Robert Livingston, chancellor (highest judicial officer) of the state of New York, administers the oath of office. "Do you solemnly swear," Livingston asks the president-elect, "that you will faithfully execute the office of president of the United States and will, to the best of your ability, preserve, protect, and defend the Constitution of the United States?"

"I do solemnly swear," Washington answers, repeating the oath, and adding, "So help me God." He bends and kisses the Bible placed before him.

"It is done!" Livingston cries out. Turning to the crowd, he shouts, "Long live George Washington, president of the United States!" The roar of the crowd rolls across the city.

The first president bows, walks back into the Sen-

Treasury Secretary Alexander Hamilton and his father-in-law, U.S. Senator Philip Schuyler of New York, stroll along Manhattan's Wall Street in 1790. At right, holding the hand of his daughter Theodosia, is future U.S. Vice-President Aaron Burr. Hamilton was killed by Burr in a duel fought in 1804.

His hand on an open Bible, Washington takes the oath of office during his inaugural ceremony at New York City's Federal Hall on April 30, 1789. At right is John Adams, first vice-president of the United States.

Wild cheering breaks out as the nation's new president appears on the balcony of New York's Federal Hall. At that moment, George Washington was by far the most popular man in America.

ate Chamber and prepares to deliver his Inaugural Address. He is a soldier, not an orator, and he is uncomfortable in this role; his voice trembles slightly. Nevertheless, he sounds a clear call for national pride, for confidence in the future of the new nation, for a sense of purpose and duty. He calls on his fellow citizens to honor "the eternal rules of order and right." He speaks reverently of the "invisible hand of the Almighty" that had guided the people to this new day. "The preservation of the sacred fire of liberty," he declares, is "staked on the experiment entrusted to the hands of the American people."

2

A Virginian

George Washington was a Virginia planter. His instincts, tastes, and beliefs had been shaped by the patterns his family had established during its three generations in the largest of Great Britain's American colonies. His forebears had worked the fields, traded in cattle, crops, and slaves; they had accumulated land and held public office. Throughout Washington's life, he remained closely attached to the land of his ancestors. He was proud of their achievements, faithful to their spirit of industry and honesty.

From the earliest clearing of forests along the James River, the character of Virginia's settlers had been influenced by the land. By the year 1700, one Virginia family in four owned from 500 to 20,000 acres. Most family units were self-sufficient. Often aided by slaves, they produced their own food, made their own clothes, built their own houses, stables, and barns. Virginia's rich land, with its thick forests, rolling hills, and gently flowing streams — "this infant, woody country," as Washington remembered it — offered great opportunities to its residents.

Washington thought of himself as a Virginian, and like many of his fellow Virginians, he thought and wrote of Virginia as "my country."
—CHARLES CECIL WALL
American historian

Washington in bronze. The towering American, one of the 18th-century world's most famous men, was constantly besieged by painters and sculptors. Washington hated to pose, but he usually obliged. The encouragement of art, he said, "is a duty which every good citizen owes to his country."

THE BETTMANN ARCHIVE

Virginia's farmers grew tobacco, wheat, and corn; some produced such supplies for the British navy as pitch, tar, and hemp. On plantations located near rivers, slaves caught fish, especially shad and herring, which were either used at home or shipped to market. Most plantations had large gardens, rich in vegetables and flowers. The life of a Virginia planter was relatively isolated, but it offered its more industrious members the chance to create an abundant existence.

George Washington's great-grandfather had come to Virginia from England in 1657. Although he arrived in the New World almost penniless, John Washington worked hard and soon acquired land and a modest fortune. He achieved a solid position in colonial Virginia, holding such offices as county coroner, tax collector, and member of the Virginia House of Burgesses, the legislature.

John Washington's grandson, Augustine Washington, owned several small plantations along the

Born in Westmoreland County, Virginia, Washington lived in this small house on the Potomac River until he was three years old. The building, which had four rooms on the first floor and several bedrooms in the steep-roofed attic, was heated by large fireplaces at either end.

Potomac River. It was at one of these, in Westmoreland County, that his second wife, Mary, gave birth to a son, George, on February 22, 1732. Several other children were born to the couple in the following years: Elizabeth in 1734, Samuel in 1735, John in 1737, and Charles in 1739.

When George was three years old, the Washingtons moved further up the Potomac River to another family tract, a spot where Little Hunting Creek empties into the Potomac. At the time, this plantation consisted only of a modest house and a few outbuildings surrounded by trees. Later the site of a magnificent home and exquisitely tended gardens, orchards, and croplands, it would be called Mount Vernon.

George's family moved again when he was six, this time to Ferry Farm, another of Augustine Washington's properties, near the little town of Fredericksburg on the Rappahannock River. Although Augustine's lands did not rank in size with those owned by Virginia's "First Families" — the Carters, Byrds, Lees, and Harrisons — he had title to several thousand acres and was master of 20 slaves. He became a justice of the peace and a sheriff, earning his neighbors' respect for his solid achievements.

In 1738 George's half-brother Lawrence returned from England, where he had been educated. Lawrence, the son of Augustine's first wife (who had died in 1729), was 20 years old, sophisticated, and charming. He soon became young George's idol.

George was privately tutored in reading, spelling, and arithmetic, for which he showed both interest and aptitude. His early school copybooks are filled with mathematical tables and notations on land surveying. Unlike Thomas Jefferson and other influential Virginians of his day, Washington neither attended the College of William and Mary in Williamsburg nor received any higher education. (He was, in fact, the only one of the nation's first six presidents who did not go to college.) He never learned French, to his later regret, and never mastered the famous works of literature and history of the time. His main interests were more physical. He loved fishing, swimming, shooting, and riding, later

Mary Ball Washington was a difficult and demanding woman who plagued her son George with endless complaints and charges of neglect. Although Washington was a national hero as well as a dutiful son, his mother never acknowledged his achievements. She died at the age of 81 in 1789.

gaining a reputation as one of the best horsemen in Virginia.

Augustine Washington died in 1743 at the age of 58. Lawrence, his eldest son, received a large portion of the inheritance, including the family farm at Little Hunting Creek. Only 11 years old when his father died, George was shuttled between the several Washington farms during his teenage years. He especially relished the company of his half-brother. Lawrence lived at the Little Hunting Creek home, which he had renamed Mount Vernon in honor of Admiral Edward Vernon, under whom he had served in the British navy. Lawrence had married Anne Fairfax, daughter of Colonel William Fairfax. Belvoir, the magnificent Fairfax estate, stood near Mount Vernon.

It was during his visits with Lawrence that young George discovered a new world, an aristocratic society of social grace, of card-playing and dancing

Washington works at the surveyor's trade. In 1748 he accompanied an expedition assigned to map the frontier lands of his wealthy neighbor, Lord Thomas Fairfax. By watching and questioning the party's surveyors, the 16-year-old learned enough to practice the profession.

THE BETTMANN ARCHIVE

Surveying or Measuring of Land

To divide a Piece of Land into three equal Parts and each Man to have the benefit of a Pond about the Middle thereof

As a teenager, Washington filled his copybooks with notes about surveying land. The future president's education was limited, but he showed skill in mathematics, which proved useful when he became the surveyor of Virginia's Culpeper County at the age of 18.

and billiards, of elegantly dressed, charming women and dashing, carefree men. The tall, muscular youngster would soon learn the ways of the wealthy and powerful.

In 1747 Belvoir heralded the arrival of one of the most powerful men in this society, Lord Thomas Fairfax. A cousin of Colonel William Fairfax, Lord Thomas was a fox-hunting English nobleman who had inherited a huge tract of land in northern Virginia between the Potomac and Rappahannock rivers. He had come to inspect his 5 million acres.

In 1748 Fairfax sent a surveying party into the

Lawrence Washington, a well-educated and glittering war hero, was the idol of his young half-brother George. Lawrence's death at the age of 36 was to make his brother master of Mount Vernon, but it was a devastating blow to the 20-year-old George.

western regions of his huge domain. He had been impressed by George Washington's skill at fox hunting, and he invited the 16-year-old to go along. The month-long trip through the backwoods was an entirely new experience for the young man, and he found it very exciting. He kept a diary in which he described swimming his horse across a snow-filled river, meeting a war party of Indians who were carrying a human scalp and who performed a war dance for the white men, encountering a rattlesnake in the woods, and spending the night at a rustic frontier lodging. There, he noted, he slept under "one Thread Bear blanket with double its Weight of Lice Flease etc."

During this trip Washington carefully observed the techniques and methods used by the experienced surveyors in the party, and he learned a great deal. A year later he helped lay out the new town of Belhaven, Virginia, later known as Alexandria. By the age of 18, he was earning his living as the surveyor of Culpeper County. With money he earned at this job, he bought his first land, 500 acres on Bullskin Creek.

Washington was also beginning to develop a strong interest in what he called the "Low Land Beauties" — the young women he was meeting at Belvoir. Although he enjoyed flirting with these "agreeable young ladies," he was not among their favorite suitors. At six feet, three inches, he was much taller than most of his contemporaries; he had unusually large hands and feet and a slow, serious speaking manner that most of the young women found too solemn for their taste. Nevertheless, he wrote a number of lovesick poems. Those that survive suggest that he was a better surveyor than he was a poet:

> From your bright sparkling Eyes, I was undone;
> Rays, you have more transparent than the Sun,
> Amidst its glory in the rising Day,
> None can you equal in your bright array . . .

As he approached his 20th birthday, Washington was thoroughly enjoying both his social and business life. Suddenly, however, a dark shadow fell across his happiness: his beloved brother Lawrence contracted tuberculosis, and his health rapidly deteriorated. Hoping that the tropical air of the Caribbean would help, the brothers visited the island of Barbados in November 1751. It was the only ocean trip George Washington ever made, and the only time he ever traveled outside what would become the United States.

The trip to Barbados helped neither brother. Lawrence grew even sicker, and George caught smallpox. Fortunately, it was a mild case and left his face only slightly scarred. It also made him immune to the dreaded disease that, during the Revolution, killed more American soldiers than did the guns of the British army.

Lawrence Washington died of tuberculosis at his Mount Vernon home in July 1752. George Washington had lost his brother, his teacher, and his best friend.

Lawrence left Mount Vernon to his daughter Sarah, with the understanding that if George outlived the girl, the estate was to go to him. Sarah died two years after her father, making George Washington master of the plantation that would always be identified with him.

The mansion at Mount Vernon was only one-and-a-half stories high when Washington inherited it. He added two floors in 1759, and continued to expand and improve it throughout his life. The magnificent final result is now open to the public.

3
Soldier

Rather than quarrel about territory, let the poor, the needy and oppressed of the earth, and those who want land, resort to the fertile plains of our western country, and there dwell in peace.
—GEORGE WASHINGTON

When George Washington was a young man, many Virginians were looking westward, dreaming of the day when settlers could move into the fertile valleys beyond the Blue Ridge Mountains. A few hardy pioneers had braved Indian attacks and carved out small frontier communities west of the mountains, but most of the Ohio River valley was still a wilderness.

It was also a potential battleground. For a century Britain and France had been struggling for supremacy and world empire. The French had established colonies in eastern Canada, and the British had settled in what is now the eastern United States. Their rivalry was becoming particularly critical in America. Both nations claimed the same Ohio Valley territory. The French had cultivated alliances with some of the area's more powerful Indian tribes and had begun to erect forts, but the land was still very much in dispute. With the British and French both determined to colonize the Ohio country, a major war seemed inevitable.

In 1753 the British government instructed Virginia Governor Robert Dinwiddie to demand that

MUSEUM OF THE AMERICAN INDIAN

Iron weapons like this one, which is part tomahawk and part tobacco pipe, were made by white craftsmen for trade with the Indians. Competing for Indian allies on the American frontier, both the French and the British engaged in extensive trade with the western tribes.

Charles Willson Peale painted Washington in the uniform of a British colonial colonel in 1772. Suspended from Washington's neck is a gorget, a gilded badge identifying its wearer as an officer. The young Virginian's exploits in service of the British during the French and Indian War made him something of a celebrity.

In Washington's youth, Virginia's Blue Ridge Mountains marked the frontier between the settled lands along the coast and the western wilderness. By the time he was 21, Washington had made several expeditions into the mountain forests.

They told me that it was their absolute design to take possession of the Ohio, and by God, they would do it.
—GEORGE WASHINGTON
on the French response to
his mission in the
Ohio Valley

the French withdraw from the forts they were constructing south of Lake Erie. If they refused, they were to be driven off by force. Young George Washington was soon in the middle of this conflict.

A year earlier Washington had received an appointment in the Virginia militia. Hearing of Dinwiddie's instructions, he volunteered to take the message to the French. The governor accepted his offer. Washington's assignment — which involved a 1,000-mile journey through snowy, trackless forests populated by hostile Indians — was fraught with danger and hazards probably not even imagined by the 21-year-old Virginian.

In November 1753 Washington set out for the West. He was accompanied by two interpreters — one who spoke French, the other who could translate the language of the local Indian tribes — and four backwoodsmen as "servitors," or helpers. Through snowstorms and driving rains, across steep mountains and treacherous rapids, the party moved slowly along, meeting with fur traders and Indians, finally reaching the French at Fort Le Boeuf (now Waterford, Pennsylvania), near Lake Erie.

Washington gathered valuable information about the French forces in the West, but his discussions with the French commander at Fort Le Boeuf were fruitless. He told Washington in no uncertain terms that the French were in the Ohio Valley to stay, and that any attempts by the English to drive them out would be repelled.

Washington returned to Virginia, accompanied by one of his interpreters. The trip was filled with harrowing incidents. Near a village known to the Indians as "Murdering Town," he and the interpreter were almost killed when their Indian guide suddenly fired at them point-blank. The Virginians sprang upon and disarmed the guide, whom the interpreter wanted to kill immediately. Washington refused to permit this act of "frontier justice"; despite his companion's protests, he set the would-be assassin free. Next, Washington and the interpreter built a log raft to ferry themselves across the ice-choked Monongahela River. Using a pole to push the rickety craft through the huge blocks of ice in the river, Washington lost his balance and pitched into the racing, icy water. He finally scrambled ashore, but his soaked clothing immediately froze solid. He spent the night rubbing snow on his frost-bitten fingers and toes.

Further on, along the bank of the Great Kanawha River, Washington and his party found the bodies of seven people who had been scalped by Indians, a gruesome sight that would be forever imprinted on Washington's mind. Finally, 11 weeks after its departure, the party returned to Virginia. Washington's report about the French refusal to abandon the Ohio Valley, and about the probability of a French attack, stunned Dinwiddie and his government.

Three months later Washington was again in the Ohio Valley. This time, he was a lieutenant colonel of Virginia troops sent to protect the men who were constructing a fort at the "Forks of the Ohio" — the junction of the Allegheny and Monongahela rivers, later the site of Pittsburgh, Pennsylvania.

Pushing west with a force of 159 men, Washington received a report that 1,000 French and Indian troops had surrounded the unfinished fort at the Forks. Although his army was vastly outnumbered, Washington proceeded toward his destination. On May 28, when he learned that a French force was encamped nearby, the brash young lieutenant colo-

Washington delivers a British message to the commander of Fort Le Boeuf, a French outpost in the Ohio Valley. The French, Washington later reported, rejected British demands that they withdraw from the area. He said they intended to seize the valley and that "by God they would do it."

nel decided to stage a surprise attack, although he had no military orders to do so. The Virginians quickly overpowered the small French party, killing 10 soldiers and capturing the rest.

Washington found this battle, the first of many he would face, exhilarating. "I have heard the bullets whistle," he said in a letter to his brother John, "and believe me, there is something charming in the sound." This minor skirmish in the forests of Pennsylvania was the opening salvo of the French and Indian War, which would drag on for eight years.

Washington's scouts now reported that a large body of French and Indian troops was marching toward him from the west, and he ordered the construction of a stockade, which he called Fort Necessity. Although he had demonstrated his courage under fire, Washington had little experience as a

Headed home from their 1753 journey into the Ohio Valley, Washington and his French interpreter pole a fragile log raft across the swollen Monongahela River. Washington soon fell into the icy water; he struggled ashore, but he nearly froze to death in the process.

military tactician. Fort Necessity, an open fortification protected only by an earthen wall and a ditch, was built in a meadow overlooked by forested hills.

The French attacked on July 3, 1754, easily overwhelming the defenders by pouring musket fire into the fort from the hills. More than a third of Washington's men had been killed or wounded when, to his amazement, the French asked for a cease-fire. Because Britain and France were not yet officially at war, the French commander decided to allow the Fort Necessity survivors to depart unharmed. Without this great dose of gallantry from the French officer, George Washington's scalp might have ended up in the possession of one of his Indian attackers — and American history might have been quite different.

When he returned to Virginia, Washington met with some criticism for the Fort Necessity defeat, but most people believed that he and his men had demonstrated great courage in the engagement. In England, the events at Fort Necessity produced an outpouring of sympathy for the defenders and a conviction that British money and arms should be dispatched to the colonies in order to drive the French from the Ohio Valley.

In the spring of 1755, two regiments of British regulars arrived in Virginia under the command of Major General Edward Braddock. Washington offered to join the British general's army as a volunteer. Braddock, delighted to have the services of a man who knew the uncharted territory he was to attack, quickly appointed the young Virginian as his personal aide.

In June 1755 Braddock's army of 1,300 men, supported by about 450 colonial soldiers, moved toward Fort Duquesne, the fortress the French had built at the Forks of the Ohio. Hacking out roads through the forest for its supply wagons and artillery, faced with illness and continued quarreling between British regulars and the companies of colonial troops, the army made excruciatingly slow progress.

After more than a month of exhausting travel, Braddock's army at last reached the Monongahela River, only seven miles from Fort Duquesne. On July

I tremble at the consequence that the defeat may have on our back settlers, who I suppose will all leave their habitations unless there are proper measures taken for their security.
—GEORGE WASHINGTON in 1775, after the defeat of Braddock's troops

31

9 the soldiers were marching along a 12-foot-wide road they had cut through the dense forest. Suddenly, a shot rang out. It was followed by the blood-curdling sound of Indian war cries, rapid bursts of gunfire — and complete pandemonium.

Jammed together in their clearing, the red-coated British soldiers were perfect targets for the French and Indian soldiers concealed among the trees. They were picked off with appalling swiftness by their unseen attackers. Panicked by the Indian war whoops, the frightened men — as Washington later remembered — "broke and run as sheep before the hounds."

Braddock, frantic and angry, rode back and forth among his terrified troops, vainly trying to rally a counterattack. Washington tried to persuade the general to lead the troops into the trees, there to "engage the enemy in their own way," but Braddock insisted on maintaining regular, parade-ground formation.

Two horses were shot from under Washington, and his jacket and hat were pierced by bullets, but he was not wounded. "The miraculous care of Providence," he later said, "protected me beyond all human expectation." Others were not as lucky. Braddock, his lung pierced by a bullet, died soon afterward. Most of the other officers and hundreds of the men were killed, their bodies lying piled atop each other at the edge of the blood-streaked road. Those who were able to move threw down their guns and fled as the whooping Indians closed in, scalping the dead and dying.

Washington later expressed his rage at the slaughter of the British troops. "We have been most scandalously beaten," he said, "by a trifling body of men." He wrote of riding through the battlefield among "shocking scenes. . . . The dead, the dying, the groans, lamentations, and cries along the road of the wounded for help . . . were enough to pierce a heart of adamant [stone]." George Washington would see many such scenes in the years ahead.

The British officers who survived Braddock's defeat publicly praised Washington's "courage and resolution." British officials, however, were seriously embarrassed by the military disaster, and they blamed it on Washington and the colonial troops. In America, there was no question about Washington's reputation after the battle on the Monongahela: he was a hero.

The British military command, deciding that the Ohio Valley was not worth further bloodshed, abandoned the area and moved its forces farther north. In Virginia, the House of Burgesses voted to rebuild the decimated Virginia Regiment to protect the colony's now undefended frontier from assault. In the fall of 1755 Washington was named "Colonel of the Virginia Regiment and Commander in Chief of all Virginia forces." He was 23 years old.

Washington was responsible for defending approximately 300 miles of mountainous frontier against the murderous incursions of French and Indian raiders, who had become even bolder after Braddock's defeat. When Washington inspected his new command at Fort Cumberland, he found chaos. Discipline was lacking, supplies short, and, worse, the feeling prevailed among the troops that the defense of Virginia was impossible.

Washington views a scene of chaos as French and Indian troops outmaneuver their British opponents during the French and Indian War. Firmly committed to traditional battle tactics, the British were often badly mauled by their opponents, who practiced what would now be called guerrilla warfare.

Washington determined to bring order and stability to his army. He sent frequent and bitter complaints to Governor Dinwiddie and the Virginia House of Burgesses about shortages of men and equipment. He described the suffering endured by the Virginian settlers on the frontier, and warned that both forts and lives would be lost if help was not forthcoming. What Washington wanted most was the authority to attack Fort Duquesne. He knew that if the French — "the fount of all our disturbance and trouble" — were driven out, most of the Indian raids would cease.

Fulfilling Washington's grim prophecies, Indian raids along the frontier became more frequent and more savage. "Nothing is to be seen or heard of," one of Washington's officers reported from Fort Cumberland, "but desolation and murder. The smoke of the burning plantations darkens the day and hides the neighboring mountains."

In the fall of 1757, Washington raced along the border he was responsible for protecting, trying to rally his forces, recruit new men, and create military order. He continued to be hampered by lack of funds and support from civilian officials, and he grew increasingly disillusioned with military service.

Washington's frantic efforts during this period taxed his strength, and in late 1757, an old illness — dysentery — returned to haunt him. He was forced to return to his home, where he lay desperately ill for four months.

In April 1758 the British, now officially at war with France, finally decided to strike another blow at Fort Duquesne. By now, Washington had resolved to resign his commission, but his health had returned and he was eager to wipe out the memory of Braddock's defeat. When a 7,000-man British army under Brigadier General John Forbes made its way to Fort Duquesne the following November, Washington and his Virginia troops were part of it.

The mission was successful, but anticlimactic. Having received reports of the advancing British army, the small French force at Duquesne burned the fort and fled. The expedition had not provided the revenge sought by the army, but it had at last driven the French from the Virginia frontier.

The war against the French continued in other parts of North America. Nevertheless, Washington carried out his resolve to return to civilian life, and he resigned his military commission at the end of 1758. The stature he had achieved among the men of his Virginia army was evident in his officers' formal farewell. They warmly praised the 26-year-old Washington's "steady adherence to impartial justice" and "invariable regard to merit," and expressed deep regret at losing his leadership. Where else, asked the officers, could they find a man "so renown't for patriotism, courage and conduct?"

Washington returned to Mount Vernon, to familiar pastimes and old friends and neighbors. As a young man, he had been a frequent guest of the wealthy and brilliant Fairfax family at Belvoir. He was especially friendly with George William, the son of Washington's employer, old William Fairfax. When Washington was 16 years old, George William

COURTESY OF MRS. SEYMOUR ST. JOHN

The love of Washington's life, Sally Fairfax, was attractive, well educated, charming—and married to his friend and neighbor, George Fairfax. Washington's passion for his dark-haired friend remained a secret until 1877, when some of his love letters were found in a trunk that had belonged to Fairfax.

George Washington and Martha Custis are married on January 6, 1759. Although Washington was never passionately in love with Custis, he was happy with her. He later observed that the most important characteristics in a mate were "good sense" and "a good disposition," both of which his wife had in abundance.

had brought home a bride, 18-year-old Sally Cary. The beautiful and witty Sally had taken young Washington under her wing, teaching him to dance, coaching him in the family's amateur theatricals, helping him to polish his manners.

As the years passed, the two friends became increasingly close. On Washington's part, the relationship was far more than a friendship, but he was able to do nothing about it beyond writing yearning letters to Sally and meeting her at polite social gatherings. A number of Washington's letters to Sally survive. In one of them, written in late 1758, he said, "Misconstrue not my meaning; doubt it not, nor expose it. The world has no business to know the object of my love declared in this manner to you, when I want to conceal it."

Three months after he wrote that note, he married Martha Custis, a plump and wealthy widow with two children. Martha's first husband had left her two mansions, an estate of more than 17,000 acres, a large amount of cash, and a number of slaves. The

wedding took place on January 6, 1759, at the Custis plantation. Martha Custis brought Washington personal warmth, a generous and cheerful nature, and a strong interest in household management. She would be a constant and faithful companion to her husband for the rest of his life.

Washington was, in turn, a loving husband to Martha and a devoted father to her children and grandchildren. But he never forgot Sally. In his last letter to her, written the year before he died at the age of 67, he told her that nothing in his life had "been able to eradicate from my mind those happy moments, the happiest of my life, which I have enjoyed in your company."

George Washington settled down to his plantation. He was what he wanted to be, a Virginia planter; he was where he wanted to be, at his beloved home along the Potomac, absorbed in his farming, enjoying the life of a prosperous landowner. He was the squire of Mount Vernon.

Returning from an inspection tour of his plantation, Washington is greeted by his wife and stepchildren, Jacky and Patsy Custis. Between 1759 and 1775, during his 16-year retirement from military service, Washington had everything he wanted: a tranquil marriage, a prosperous farm, a handsome home, and a hand in local and national politics.

4

From Planter to Revolutionary

After his retirement from the army, Washington spent 16 years at Mount Vernon, engaged in the activities he loved. Strong and athletic, a fine dancer and extraordinary horseman, Washington hunted, bred horses and dogs, attended balls, plays, and horse races. He enlarged the mansion at Mount Vernon, redesigned its gardens, and, with Martha, lavishly entertained crowds of friends and political associates. In 1758 he was elected to the Virginia House of Burgesses.

Washington was a skilled administrator and a shrewd businessman; he ably managed both Mount Vernon and Martha's vast properties, and added considerably to his wife's fortune. He also steadily acquired more acreage, even buying the land where the ill-fated Fort Necessity had once stood.

Washington never fathered any children, but he was an affectionate stepfather to Martha's two, Martha ("Patsy") and John ("Jacky") Custis. Patsy died of epilepsy at the age of 17. Jacky, a pleasure-loving young man with few interests beyond horses and clothes, resisted all his stepfather's efforts to edu-

At a time when our lordly masters in Great Britain will be satisfied with nothing less than the deprivation of American freedom, it seems highly necessary that something should be done to avert the stroke and maintain the liberty which we have derived from our ancestors.
—GEORGE WASHINGTON during the Stamp Act crisis

"Washington the Farmer," a painting by American artist N. C. Wyeth, shows the future president taking notes as he checks on crop production at Mount Vernon. Fascinated by agriculture, Washington not only read everything he could about the subject, he experimented with seeds, soils, fertilizers, and irrigation techniques.

George III of England. After Britain's heavy losses in Boston, Washington expected the king to curb the expanding conflict. The British ruler, however, was infuriated by the defiance of the American "traitors." Instead of attempting to prevent war, he announced he would hire mercenary troops to crush the colonists' insurrection.

cate him. He had no desire to learn how to manage his family's estates or to enter military service. "I never in my life did know," reported Jacky's exasperated tutor to Washington, "a youth so exceedingly indolent, or so surprisingly voluptuous; one would suppose Nature had intended him for some Asiatic prince." When Jacky died at the age of 27, George and Martha Washington adopted the two youngest of his four children.

On the plantation, Washington eagerly read the latest books from London about new agricultural methods, and he put many of them to the test at Mount Vernon. Tobacco, most of which was shipped overseas, had traditionally been the main cash crop of the plantation. According to British law, however, American planters could ship goods to England only on English ships. After making a thorough study of his accounts, Washington realized that the costs of English freight, English insurance, and English import duties wiped out almost all the profit he made on his American tobacco.

Accordingly, he switched to raising wheat, which he could sell in nearby Alexandria, Virginia. This crop proved to be extremely profitable, and he went on to experiment with alfalfa, buckwheat, flax, and hemp. He also built a new mill for grinding his own and (at a profit) his neighbors' grain, and he increased the fishing operations on his land. He was soon exporting barrels of fish as well as large quantities of linen and wool cloth woven on the estate.

This, then, was George Washington in his comfortable Virginia setting — respected, successful, building a considerable fortune. But events of a larger scale would soon launch the Virginia planter into a new arena. He would find himself amidst the perilous drift of the American colonies toward revolution.

The French and Indian War had ended in 1763 with the signing of the Treaty of Paris. The treaty had given to Great Britain almost all of the North American continent previously controlled by the French. Britain's King George III now reigned over the world's mightiest empire. But the war in America had been long and expensive, doubling the British national debt. Taxes in Britain were high, and many Britons felt that the colonies in America were not paying their fair share.

In 1765 the British Parliament passed the Stamp Act, which required the American colonists to buy tax stamps for most printed matter, from newspapers to playing cards, from deeds of sale to marriage licenses. The act outraged many Americans. Since the colonists were not represented in the British Parliament, the Americans insisted that the measure was taxation without representation. No one had the right to tax Americans, they argued, but their own elected legislators.

In the House of Burgesses, Virginia's most eloquent orator, Patrick Henry, made a fiery speech against the Stamp Act. When he suggested that, like other "tyrants" before him, George III might even lose his head, cries of "Treason!" were heard in the assembly. "If *this* be treason," retorted the defiant Henry, "make the most of it!" Henry's words dazzled the burgesses. Thomas Jefferson later credited him with setting in motion "the ball of revolution."

Henry's speech was only one of the passionate salvos fired against the British by their American subjects. Even George Washington, whose remarks in the assembly had been few and moderate until now, spoke up with anger. Parliament, he declared, "hath no more right to put their hands into my pocket, without my consent, than I have to put my hands into yours for money."

Backing down in the face of this strong colonial resistance, the British government repealed the Stamp Act in early 1766. But the lull in tension

They that can give up essential liberty to obtain a little temporary safety deserve neither liberty nor safety.
—BENJAMIN FRANKLIN
American patriot, scientist, and philosopher, in 1759

Bostonians take to the streets to protest "taxation without representation," represented by the British-imposed Stamp Act of 1765. Few British moves so outraged Americans; in every colony, riots broke out in which official stamp paper was destroyed, tax collectors hanged in effigy, and customs offices burned.

Taunted to the breaking point, British soldiers in Boston open fire on a crowd of Americans on March 5, 1770. Five people were killed; one of them was Crispus Attucks, the first black to die in the revolutionary cause. The "Boston Massacre" pushed the colonies even further toward a firm break with Britain.

Our cause is noble, it is the cause of mankind!
—GEORGE WASHINGTON
on the American colonists'
struggle against the British

between the colonies and the British was short-lived. The relationship had become a test of wills, and the British were determined to assert their authority over the colonists.

In 1767 Parliament passed the Townshend Acts, which placed import duties on such items as paper, glass, paint, ink, and tea. London insisted that these measures, unlike the Stamp Act, were not internal taxes but external ones — that is, the taxes on goods were to be collected at the ports where they entered the country, rather than within the country. Regardless of the fine distinction the British made between the types of taxes, the Townshend Acts heightened colonial anger. The cries of protest became louder.

In a letter to his friend and fellow planter George Mason, Washington said, "At a time when our lordly masters in Great Britain will be satisfied with nothing less than the deprivation of American freedom, it seems highly necessary that something should be done to avert the stroke and maintain the liberty which we have derived from our ancestors."

Washington was present on the day in 1769 when the Virginia House of Burgesses adopted resolutions aimed against the British Parliament's right to tax. The resolutions demanded that the people of Virginia — not members of Parliament sitting across the ocean — should decide what taxes should be raised in Virginia and for what purposes. Acting for the British crown in the dispute, Virginia's colonial governor quickly retaliated by dissolving the House of Burgesses.

The angry burgesses soon reassembled in the Apollo Room of the Raleigh Tavern in Williamsburg. There, they entered into an agreement, pledging to buy no goods taxed by Parliament. The agreement was designed to hurt British merchants, thus forcing Parliament to repeal the Townshend Acts. Washington fully supported the nonimportation agreements. If petitions and words could not persuade the British to change their taxation policies, he said, perhaps "starving their trade and manufactures" would be more effective.

In the months that followed, similar agreements were drawn up in other colonies. In Massachusetts, under the leadership of such men as Samuel Otis and Samuel Adams — men who were calling themselves "Sons of Liberty" — discontent was especially strong. Once again, the British bowed to the rising pressure, removing all the taxes except for the one on tea. Not even this gesture, however, reduced the growing hostility between the mother country and the colonists. As long as the tax on tea remained in

American patriots toss expensive British tea into Boston Harbor on December 16, 1773. The "Boston Tea Party" was a deliberate attempt to provoke the British. Harsh reprisals against the colonies would, the patriots predicted, unite the colonists against Britain. The mission was a success.

force, the colonists would feel aggrieved.

In Massachusetts, colonial anger reached violent levels and brought tragedy. On a cold evening in March 1770 a group of noisy men and boys began to pelt the British sentries at the customs house with snowballs. Insults flew, then stones and bullets. When the smoke cleared, three townspeople were dead and two lay mortally wounded in the snow. Across America, word of the "Boston Massacre" spread. The conflict had reached frightening proportions.

In the face of what they saw as British tyranny, the colonial assemblies now formed "committees of correspondence" to enable the restless colonies to keep in close touch with one another. In these early committees were the seeds of a united front against the British, the beginnings of a widespread revolt against the mother country.

Most colonial leaders still believed that the dispute could be resolved, that they could reassert their own rights as Englishmen and continue to live under British rule. But events were moving the two sides toward an unhealable rupture.

In December 1773 a group of Americans disguised as Mohawk Indians gathered at Boston's harbor, boarded three British merchant ships, and dumped their cargo of tea into the water. The "Boston Tea Party," a gesture of outrage against the tax on tea, shocked the British. "The die is now cast," thundered King George. "The colonies must either submit or perish."

When the colonists refused to pay for the tea they had destroyed, Parliament passed a new set of acts. One of them closed the port of Boston, another sharply reduced the rights of self-government in Massachusetts, and a third one — the "Quartering Act" — forced colonists to provide lodging in their homes for British troops. The "Intolerable Acts," as these measures were called by Americans, killed the last hope of reconciliation between the colonies and the mother country.

The rift between Britain and America also divided friends in the colonies. Washington, for example, told his neighbor Bryan Fairfax that the money involved with the British tax on tea was not important. The issue, he said, was the right of the colonies to vote on their own taxes. Fairfax responded by expressing his impatience with the "broils and revolutions" concocted by American radicals. But Washington maintained that the time had come when "we must assert our rights, or submit . . . till custom and use shall make us . . . tame and abject slaves." In public Washington was still saying little about the growing conflict; in private he was taking an increasingly strong position against the British colonial policy.

In June 1774 a small group of lawyers led by Patrick Henry and Richard Henry Lee met at the Raleigh Tavern to show their solidarity with the Massachusetts patriots. The Virginians proposed that the committees of correspondence in all the colonies appoint delegates to meet in a Continental Congress. The idea was accepted enthusiastically by the other colonies.

To represent itself in the First Continental Congress, which was to be held in Philadelphia, Virginia chose seven men. One of them was George Washington. On the last day of August 1774, he and Patrick Henry took a ferry across the Potomac and headed north.

Philadelphia was the most important city in America, its center for art and science. Here on the bluffs overlooking the Schuylkill and Delaware rivers, delegates from America's 13 colonies walked the cobblestoned streets, talking about the escalating conflict with Britain, debating about action.

What did these men, each representing a separate part of America, each with different interests and different cultures, have in common? How could they work together in harmony? When he first arrived in Philadelphia, John Adams of Massachusetts wrote to his wife Abigail that the delegates were "fifty strangers . . . jealous of each other, fearful, timid, skittish."

As the deliberations began, however, it became clear that the delegates were united by a powerful bond: their unshakable opposition to British policy. Washington's colleague Patrick Henry electrified the

Flanked by Governor Edmund Pendleton of Virginia and revolutionary orator Patrick Henry, Washington rides toward Philadelphia, site of the First Continental Congress, in early September 1774.

If you speak of solid information and sound judgment, Colonel Washington is unquestionably the greatest man on the floor.
—PATRICK HENRY
American patriot,
during the First
Continental Congress

Benjamin Franklin published this drawing in his newspaper, the *Pennsylvania Gazette*, on May 9, 1754. The snake's sections represent the 13 American colonies, although Delaware is inexplicably left out. The New England colonies — Massachusetts, Connecticut, Rhode Island, and New Hampshire — are shown as the head of the serpent. The message is clear.

Congress when he declared, "I am not a Virginian but an American."

Peyton Randolph, another of Washington's Virginia colleagues, was chosen as president of the Congress. Washington himself impressed many of the delegates, not with a flood of words, but with his commanding presence and his reputation as a gifted military leader. Connecticut delegate Silas Deane noted that Washington spoke "very modestly, and in a cool, but determined style."

After roundly condemning Britain's tax measures and writing an agreement to refuse to import British goods, the First Continental Congress adjourned in October 1774. It scheduled its next meeting for the following May. What would the next half-year bring? When Washington returned to Mount Vernon, talk of armed conflict had become common. As counties across Virginia began organizing military companies, as young boys began to march and drill, Washington felt war in the air.

Its first shots were not long in coming. Outside Boston, on the road between Lexington and Concord, groups of Massachusetts militia who called themselves "Minutemen" clashed with the scarlet columns of British troops. Many died. A Salem, Massachusetts, newspaper reported, "Last Wednesday, the 19th of April, the troops of his Britannick Majesty commenced hostilities upon the people of this province . . . we are involved in all the horror of a civil war. . . ." When news of the battle reached him, Washington wrote of his great sorrow in learning "that a brother's sword has been sheathed in a brother's breast."

In early May Washington returned to Philadelphia for the Second Continental Congress. He wore the red and blue colors of the Virginia Regiment, the uniform he had worn during the French and Indian War. The gesture told his fellow delegates that he believed the time for military action had arrived.

Just after Washington reached Philadelphia, a group of colonists led by Ethan Allen and Benedict Arnold seized a large supply of arms and artillery from a British garrison at Fort Ticonderoga, near Quebec. Two weeks later, the British frigate *Cerberus* dropped anchor in Boston Harbor; aboard were three important passengers, William Howe, Henry Clinton, and John Burgoyne. They were British generals, sent to tame the American upstarts. The skirmishes of early spring were giving way to full-scale military confrontation.

The Continental Congress was now ready to raise an army to defend the colonies against the British power. That army would need a commander. As the delegates contemplated the possibilities, the choice seemed clear. Among them was a man of great physical stature, a man of experience in military leadership, one who had fought Frenchmen, who had fought Indians, a man whom everyone seemed to notice even though he said relatively little. On June 14 John Adams proposed that Congress appoint as the commander in chief "a gentleman from Virginia." George Washington was then unanimously elected by the delegates.

Writing to his wife, Washington said, "It has been determined in Congress, that the whole army raised for the defense of the American cause shall be put under my care . . . as it has been a kind of destiny that has thrown me upon this service, I shall hope that my undertaking is designed to answer some good purpose."

I am ready to raise 1,000 men, subsist them myself at my own expense, and march at their head to Boston.
—GEORGE WASHINGTON

5

Commander in Chief

For the commander in chief of their armies, the Americans needed a man with a high sense of purpose, one who exuded confidence and inspired trust. Washington was the ideal choice for the job. He was "no harum-scarum, ranting, swearing fellow," one congressional delegate said, "but sober, steady, and calm." Although he told the Continental Congress he did not think himself "equal to the command," Washington seemed to have been born for the position of leadership in which he suddenly found himself.

A week after his appointment, the new commander set out for Boston, scene of the growing hostilities. With him were his two subordinates, Major Generals Charles Lee and Horatio Gates.

As Washington's party passed through New York City, an express rider brought the news of a major battle between British Redcoats and colonial militia. It had been fought on June 17 at Breed's Hill (usually misidentified as Bunker Hill) in Charlestown, outside Boston. The Americans had lost 441 men and been driven away from the hill, but the British had suffered tremendous casualties. They lost

I am embarked on a wide ocean, boundless in its prospect and in which, perhaps, no safe harbor is to be found.
—GEORGE WASHINGTON
after his appointment as commander in chief of the Continental Army

Appointed commander in chief of the Continental Army in June 1775, Washington faced a monumental task. Said one sympathetic observer, "I pity our poor general, who has a greater burden on his shoulders and more difficulties to struggle with than should fall to the share of so good a man."

1,054 men — nearly half of their attacking force and one-fifth of their total army. (Reporting to King George, British General Thomas Gage wrote: "The loss we have sustained is greater than we can bear . . . I wish this cursed place was burned.")

When Washington arrived in Cambridge, Massachusetts, in early July 1775, the Americans were attempting to drive the remainder of Gage's Redcoats from nearby Boston. Washington hoped that a quick victory would send an undeniable message to London — that Britain must come to just terms with its American subjects.

He was in for a rude awakening. His "Continental Army" consisted of about 15,000 men, most of whom were untrained and undisciplined. Their officers had little notion of authority. Their camps were filthy and disorganized. The men lacked supplies and they were underpaid.

As he had done years earlier on the Virginia frontier, Washington began to whip his army into shape. He demanded reinforcements, and they arrived: 13

Before photography was invented, on-the-scene artists supplied visual information to newspapers. This illustration was captioned "Attack on Bunker's Hill, with the Burning of Charlestown." The Battle of Bunker (actually Breed's) Hill was technically an American defeat, but the British losses far outweighed those suffered by the Continental Army.

companies from Pennsylvania, Maryland, and Virginia, armed with long-barreled rifles. He managed to get more food, medicine, tents, and guns. He instituted stricter discipline. Still, the new commander despaired: "Could I have foreseen what I have, and am likely to experience," he wrote, "no consideration upon earth should have induced me to accept this command."

Washington warned Congress in September that the whole concept of the Continental Army must be changed. The soldiers must be offered reasonable pay and must be enlisted for longer periods. Holding a ragtag group of militiamen on short-term enlistment was, Washington insisted, an almost impossible task. It was one with which he would struggle throughout the war.

In proportion as the structure of a government gives force to public opinion, it is essential that public opinion be enlightened.
—GEORGE WASHINGTON

Although Washington hated inactivity, his army was not yet ready for an offensive against the British troops occupying Boston. He was forced to wait out the winter at his Cambridge headquarters.

Many Americans still hoped for reconciliation with the mother country, but enthusiasm for independence was mounting. That sentiment was increased in January 1776, when a pamphlet called *Common Sense* began to circulate among the colonists. Written by Thomas Paine, a recent immigrant from England, the tract proved to be political dynamite. "It burst from the press with an effect which has rarely been produced by type or paper in any age or country," wrote Philadelphia physician Benjamin Rush.

In *Common Sense*, Paine searingly attacked the British monarchy, insisting that there was "something very absurd in supposing a continent can be perpetually governed by an island." Paine demanded immediate independence from Britain: "The blood of the slain," he roared, "the weeping voice of nature cries, 'Tis Time to Part!' "

Washington called Paine's arguments "sound doctrine and unanswerable reasoning." And it was on Washington and the ragged army he commanded that everything — all this growing talk of independence, all this revolutionary fervor, all this speculation about America's future — depended.

In March 1776 Washington made his first major move of the war. Henry Knox, a one-time Boston bookseller who served as Washington's artillery commander, had obtained 60 cannon from Ticonderoga, the British fort in northern New York that had recently fallen to American forces. Loading the big guns aboard ox-drawn sledges, Knox and his men had dragged them through 200 miles of icy, mountainous wilderness. In late February they arrived at Washington's Cambridge headquarters with their welcome burden. The American army was now ready to challenge the British in Boston.

On the night of March 4, 3,000 soldiers from Washington's army quietly carried fortification materials — and Knox's cannon — onto the steep hills of the Dorchester peninsula, overlooking Boston. The following morning, General William Howe, now in charge of the British forces in Boston, awoke to a shock. Looming above him were two immense batteries, their fearful cannon aimed at his troops.

Howe had no intention of staying within such close range of the enemy's guns. Raising a white flag, he sent a runner to Washington with a message: the Americans could have Boston in return for the safe evacuation of the British troops. Washington agreed, and Howe dumped his own cannon into the harbor and set sail for Nova Scotia. George Washington had won his first victory without fighting a battle. But he knew that this British retreat was only temporary.

On July 4, 1776, the rebellion was given new meaning. "We hold these truths to be self-evident, that all men are created equal," resounded the bold phrases of Thomas Jefferson in the Declaration of Independence, "that they are endowed by their Creator with certain inalienable Rights, that among these are Life, Liberty, and the pursuit of Happiness." The Declaration, which concluded by affirming that the American colonies were now "Free and Independent States," turned the rebellion into a war for independence.

Washington had taken his army to New York, which he expected to be the next objective of the British forces. On the evening of July 9, at Wash-

> *Tyranny, like hell, is not easily conquered.*
>
> —THOMAS PAINE
> political philosopher and
> author of *Common Sense*

Thomas Paine's stirring essay *Common Sense* created a sensation in the revolutionary America of 1776. Even those Americans (Washington was among them) who had believed in the possibility of coming to terms with Britain were converted by Paine's powerful argument for complete independence.

ington's order, the Declaration of Independence was read to the troops in New York. The cheering men fired muskets and cannon, and soon the entire city joined the celebration. Crashing down came the city's statue of King George III. (Most of the statue's fragments were later sent to Connecticut, where they were melted into bullets to be used against George's troops.)

And what of the king himself? In the eyes of George III, Thomas Jefferson and the other signers of the Declaration of Independence, along with such "arch-rebels" as George Washington, were all traitors who deserved to be hanged. The British monarch was determined to crush the American Revolution. To this end, he augmented his forces in America with 10,000 hired soldiers — mercenaries — from Germany. The king was not about to let these "rebellious Americans" establish "an independent empire" in *his* domain!

As Washington had foreseen, the first major British thrust was at New York City. The British hoped to seize the city, which would enable them to gain control of the Hudson River and isolate New England from the rest of the states. New York was extremely vulnerable, and the British had almost complete control of the sea; Washington knew that defending his position would be almost impossible. "We expect a very bloody summer of it at New York," he wrote. In July ships of the British navy began to appear in New York's harbor. As the Americans watched in growing alarm, one troopship after another sailed in, bringing General Howe's men from Nova Scotia and thousands of fresh reinforcements from Europe. By the time all his forces were assembled, Howe had 30,000 seasoned troops. Washington had 23,000, most of them inexperienced and poorly armed.

An uneasy calm prevailed for several weeks. In late August Howe broke the suspense by landing large numbers of his troops on Long Island. He quickly moved them to Brooklyn Heights, across the East River from Manhattan Island. Washington had built strong fortifications on Brooklyn Heights but, worried about leaving Manhattan unprotected, he had divided his forces; half his troops were on Manhattan, half of them on Long Island.

After inflicting many casualties on the American defenders in Brooklyn, Howe's troops outflanked them. The Americans were now stranded in their fortifications; on one side of them was Howe's army and on the other the East River, filled with Howe's warships. To the British, the defeat of the enemy seemed inevitable.

Two days later, however, that enemy had disappeared. Under cover of darkness and fog, Washington had secretly evacuated 9,000 soldiers from Long Island. A fleet of small boats, crossing and recrossing the East River all night long, had silently ferried the men from Brooklyn to Manhattan.

The Battle of Brooklyn Heights had cost Washington 1,500 men, but the rest of his army was safe, at least for the moment. It had been a daring maneuver, one that even the British conceded had "a high place among military transactions."

In the next few weeks, the two sides engaged in a series of hit-and-run battles around New York and New Jersey. Washington's forces won a few skirmishes, but they were more often defeated than victorious. Because of many battlefield casualties, desertions, and the departures of soldiers whose brief enlistments were up, Washington's army was now reduced to 7,000 men. The British forces, numerous, well disciplined, and well armed, clearly had the upper hand over the tattered Americans.

Washington was well known for his calm, even disposition. That reputation, however, owed more to the towering Virginian's self-control than to his natural temperament. In the wretched, weary months that followed his retreat from Long Island, Washington's iron self-discipline was tested more severely than at any time in his life. He was exhausted, criticized for failing to achieve quick success, beset by his troops' frequent unwillingness to fight. On more than one occasion, he chased fleeing American soldiers, lashing out at them with his riding crop and shouting vain orders.

At one point, Washington ordered a band of inexperienced militiamen to stand and fight a contingent of attacking British troops. The panicked Americans ignored him, dropped their guns, and ran for their lives. White with fury, Washington hurled his hat to the ground, roaring "Good God! Are these the men with whom I am to defend America?" Alone, a tall target on horseback, he stayed to face the onrushing enemy.

Luckily, some American officers nearby saw what was happening and pulled their general to safety. One of them, Nathanael Greene, later wrote that Washington had been "so vexed at the infamous conduct of his troops that he sought death rather than life." Whatever trials he later faced, Washington would never again reveal so much of his own fiery nature.

In November Washington divided his army, leaving garrisons along New York's Hudson River to protect New England from the British. With barely 2,000 men, he then crossed the Hudson into New

This contemporary sketch of "A Real American Rifleman" was based more on optimism than reality. Although Congress had passed regulations on soldiers' dress, complete uniforms were scarce in Washington's army. Most enlisted men wore ordinary clothes, augmented by whatever scraps of military gear they could find.

Aroused by the words of the newly signed Declaration of Independence, New Yorkers pull down the city's statue of George III in July 1776. George's statue was later melted down into bullets for the Continental Army.

Jersey, heading for Philadelphia, the nation's capital. After miles of cold, dispiriting marching, Washington's threadbare army reached the Delaware River and crossed into Pennsylvania early in December. The pursuing British army arrived at the river just as the last boatload of Americans left the shore.

Washington was by now, he confessed, "wearied almost to death." There seemed to be nothing to prevent the Redcoats from marching on Philadelphia. Aware of this gloomy prospect, the Continental Congress withdrew from the city and took refuge in Baltimore. With many in Washington's army deserting, with winter coming on, with American spirit and fortunes lagging sorely, the "game," as Washington put it, seemed "pretty near up."

Washington was down, but by no means out. Now, with one bold stroke he turned a collection of ragged and discouraged men into a powerful fighting machine.

General Howe had decided to quarter most of his troops in New York for the winter, but he left several garrisons in New Jersey. One of these posts, manned by several thousand German mercenaries, was at Trenton, just across the Delaware River from Washington's base in Pennsylvania. Washington knew the British thought his army was too weak to threaten them, and he knew that the last thing they expected was a midwinter attack. He decided to surprise them.

Christmas Day, 1776, was bitter cold; by evening a fierce northeast wind was carrying sheets of hail and snow. At eight o'clock that night, Washington marched 2,400 men — some of them without coats or shoes — through the blizzard to the ferry landing, nine miles from their camp. There, they boarded barges, and, with their horses and cannon, poled their way across the ice-choked Delaware. When they reassembled on the New Jersey side at three in the morning, one officer reported that his men's weapons and powder were soaked and unusable. Washington's response was quick. "Use the bayonet," he said. "I am determined to take Trenton."

And take it he did. The enemy soldiers, sleepy and astonished, surrendered in short order. Two American soldiers froze to death en route to the battle and four were wounded, but none was killed by the enemy. The raid netted almost 1,000 prisoners, six huge brass cannon, hundreds of small arms, a storehouse of supplies — and a massive infusion of confidence for the Americans. "All our hopes," the

Washington's troops evacuate Long Island in August 1776. Surrounded by the British, Washington had ordered a silent, nightlong ferry operation to move his men to safety. When British General William Howe moved in for the kill, he was shocked to find the rebel army gone.

British secretary of war later commented, "were blasted by the unhappy affair at Trenton."

Shortly before the attack, Washington had read these words by Thomas Paine in his periodical, *Crisis*: "These are the times that try men's souls. The summer soldier and the sunshine patriot will, in this crisis, shrink from the service of their country; but he that stands it now, deserves the love and thanks of man and woman. . . . The harder the conflict the more glorious the triumph. . . ." Washington ordered Paine's words read to his men. They had proved they were no longer "summer soldiers," and their recent actions had, said their leader, given him "inexpressible pleasure."

Washington followed up the Trenton victory by attacking a British force at Princeton. Again, his army won the day. For the first time in the war, a British force broke and ran from the Americans. Mounted on his huge white horse, Washington led his men in pursuit of the enemy, shouting, "It's a fine fox chase, my boys!" With this success under their belts, the Americans quietly withdrew into winter quarters in the hills around Morristown, New Jersey.

The events of late 1776 had not only revitalized the army, they had begun to establish the legend of George Washington, the country's savior. Stories about the tall Virginian, some of them true, some wildly exaggerated, sprang up throughout the states. Many of them were based on his apparent invulnerability to bullets. Indeed, although he took great risks and was often exposed, as one of his officers noted, "to the hottest fire of the enemy," he was never wounded.

During the attack on Princeton, for example, Washington rode ahead of his troops; as they approached the British, both sides opened fire. An aide later recalled covering his eyes to spare himself the sight of the general's death. When he next looked, many soldiers were dead, but their leader was unharmed, still astride his tall horse.

After Trenton and Princeton, wrote one Virginian in his journal, "Washington's name is extolled to the clouds." In his later years, Washington was often

> *He is the greatest man on earth.*
>
> —ROBERT MORRIS
> American financier and politician, after Washington's victory at Trenton

followed by people trying simply to touch him, as though his "magic" might rub off.

Washington's army, inferior in numbers, had out of necessity become a mobile force, moving from one location to another quickly, fighting only when necessary or when the situation was strategically favorable. The object was to survive, to keep the army intact, to wear down the enemy's patience, to keep the revolution alive.

Washington still hoped to build an army whose soldiers were enlisted for long terms. Only seasoned and disciplined troops, he believed, could muster the kind of offensive necessary to defeat the British. For now, his troops were more an annoyance than an actual threat to the Redcoats. But Washington kept the Continental Army on its feet, kept up their spirits, kept them together.

The Americans did have several advantages: they were fighting on their home soil; they were receiving some men and supplies from France and Spain, England's ancient enemies; their enemy was less strongly motivated than they were. The costly conflict was generally unpopular in England. Trying to

At the head of a flotilla of troop-filled barges, Washington crosses the Delaware River on Christmas Day, 1776. His objective was Trenton, New Jersey, where a large contingent of German mercenary troops was encamped. Taking the enemy by surprise, the Americans achieved one of the war's most impressive victories.

run a war 3,000 miles away, with erratic communications and huge problems in supplying troops, was difficult and confusing. Washington believed that if he could hold on, the British might become weary of the whole enterprise.

Far from giving up their frustrating war, however, the British were preparing for a major campaign. What they were up to was a mystery to the Americans. Howe had pulled most of his forces out of northern New Jersey in the spring of 1777. In June he loaded his army onto naval transports, raising a crucial question. Was he on his way to join British General John Burgoyne, whose army was heading toward New England from Canada? Or would he move the other way, and attack Philadelphia?

Responding to contradictory information from his spies, Washington marched his army first

Washington's headquarters at Valley Forge, the windy plateau where the Continental Army spent the bitterly cold winter of 1777–78. Deeply concerned about the plight of his men, who lacked warm clothing, food, and medicine, Washington pleaded with Congress for supplies, but it was almost spring before he got them.

north, then south. He was heading back toward New York in August when he learned that the British fleet carrying Howe's troops was sailing through Chesapeake Bay, obviously to invade Philadelphia.

The Americans raced back to the capital. On September 11 two armies met at Brandywine Creek, about 20 miles outside Philadelphia. Washington's 11,000 men, exhausted by their constant marching through the summer's sweltering heat, were out-maneuvered and outfought by Howe's 18,000 rested, well-trained troops. On September 26 Howe entered Philadelphia. Congress, which had returned to the capital after its earlier flight, again vacated the city, this time to York, Pennsylvania.

In early October Washington launched a surprise attack against the British at Germantown, a settlement just outside Philadelphia. After a sharp fight, the Americans, hampered by a thick fog, a shortage of ammunition, and heavy casualties, were forced to retreat.

By now Washington's military skills were highly respected both by his British enemy and by other nations, particularly France. In his own country, however, his reputation plummeted after his defeats at Brandywine and Germantown. The man hailed as the nation's savior only a few months earlier was now being called "slack," "remiss," and "weak." The man of the hour was General Horatio Gates, the "hero of Saratoga."

General Burgoyne's 6,000-man army had received a crushing defeat at Saratoga, New York, on October 17. Although the American victory was largely due to the skill and courage of Benedict Arnold, Gates, as the senior officer, received credit. America's failure to recognize Arnold's triumph would later bear bitter fruit.

In spite of Burgoyne's defeat, Philadelphia, America's capital and its largest city, was now firmly in control of the British army. There it would stay for the winter of 1777–78.

Meanwhile, Washington took his own army into winter quarters. The site he selected for his camp was a windswept plateau 18 miles north of Philadelphia. It was known as Valley Forge.

Although he was surrounded by officers and citizens, it was impossible to mistake for a moment his majestic figure.
—MARQUIS DE LAFAYETTE
French statesman, on first seeing Washington in 1777

6

From Valley Forge to Victory

The winter of 1777–78 was a miserable time for the American army at Valley Forge. Housed in drafty wooden huts, the men were cold, hungry, often without coats or even shoes. They were beset with illnesses, including smallpox and typhus, but medical supplies were almost nonexistent. A visiting congressional delegation reported that "the skeleton of an army presented itself to our eyes in a naked starving condition, out of health, out of spirits."

One of the army's few doctors wrote of a typical sight at Valley Forge: "There comes a soldier, his bare feet are seen through his worn-out shoes, his legs nearly naked from the tattered remains of an only pair of stockings, his breeches not sufficient to cover his nakedness, his shirt hanging in strings. He comes and cries with an air of wretchedness and despair, 'I am sick, my feet lame, my legs are sore, my body covered with this tormenting itch. . . .' "

Washington bombarded Congress with requests for aid for his men. "There are now in this army," one of his letters raged, "4,000 men wanting blankets, near 2,000 of which have never had one, altho'

> *Naked and starving as they are, we cannot enough admire the incomparable patience and fidelity of the soldiery.*
> —GEORGE WASHINGTON
> on the army at Valley Forge

Men of Washington's army seek relief from the icy blasts of the Valley Forge winter. The army's clothing supplies were almost nonexistent; soldiers not lucky enough to own a pair of tattered boots and a ragged blanket walked coatless and barefoot in the snow.

Washington confers with Lafayette at Valley Forge. The American general admired few of the European officers who offered their services to the Revolution — he once called them "hungry adventurers" — but he considered Lafayette both a valiant soldier and a good friend.

some of them have been 12 months in service." Another letter to Congress angrily noted that "it is a much easier and less distressing thing to draw remonstrances in a comfortable room by a good fireside than to occupy a cold, bleak hill, and sleep under frost and snow." His tone changed at the end of the letter: "From my soul," he said, "I pity these miseries, which it is neither in my power to relieve or prevent."

Mismanagement and inefficiency were partly to blame for Congress's failure to aid the suffering men at Valley Forge. Also contributing to the problem was a lack of reliable currency. Tradesmen and farmers were reluctant to accept payment for their goods in the virtually worthless money issued by the Continental Congress. Congress responded to one of Washington's entreaties by suggesting that he collect his own supplies at gunpoint from the local citizenry. This, not surprisingly, the general refused to do.

The army persevered through the long days of winter. Still, few supplies arrived. A year earlier Washington had read Thomas Paine's words to his men: "These are the times that try men's souls. . . ." Surely now, here at this place, at this time, their souls were being sorely tested. The fact that the soldiers neither mutinied nor deserted in large numbers is remarkable, a testament to the loyalty that Washington inspired.

Washington continued to fire off furious letters to Congress, and the situation gradually improved. By March 12 Washington could write that the army was at last "pretty well supplied."

Along with food, clothing, medicine, and equipment, the Americans welcomed the arrival of a new man. He was, he said, Baron von Steuben, a former lieutenant general in the service of Frederick the Great of Prussia. The 47-year-old Steuben turned out to be neither a baron nor an ex-officer of high rank. He was, however, a seasoned military veteran and an expert drillmaster, and he proved to be a great asset to the bedraggled American army.

For a long time Washington had fretted about his soldiers' lack of military know-how; Steuben taught them the fundamentals of military drill, maneuvers, the use of bayonets, and other arts of war. Washington, deeply impressed by the Prussian's zeal and knowledge, recommended him for a commission in the Continental Army. Appointed a major general, Steuben became the army's inspector general, and the army became a better fighting force.

In early May Washington received happy news: France had recognized the independence of the United States, and had signed a treaty of alliance with the new nation. "No event," wrote Washington, "was ever received with more heartfelt joy."

The alliance, forged through the diplomatic efforts of American agents Benjamin Franklin and

Galloping up to General Charles Lee (right) at Monmouth Court House, New Jersey, Washington shouts, "What is all this confusion for, and retreat?" Lee's rambling excuses for fleeing the battle were met, reported one witness, by a torrent of curses from the commander in chief.

Silas Deane, had as its aim American "liberty, sovereignty, and independence, absolute and unlimited." Washington knew that the alliance with the French could make the critical difference in the war. Other European countries would follow France's lead. The Americans were no longer alone in their drive for independence.

The American cause was enormously popular in France. The French government saw an independent United States as a tool it could use against the hated British, and many private French citizens were deeply sympathetic to the ideals of the American revolutionists. Washington received countless offers of service from French military officers. The most important of these volunteers was the Marquis de Lafayette, who came to the United States in 1777.

Idealistic and passionately dedicated to liberty, this wealthy young nobleman had arrived in his own ship, eager to put it and himself at the service of the Americans. Congress quickly commissioned him as a major general and assigned him to Washington's staff.

The 20-year-old Frenchman and the 45-year-old American liked each other immediately. Determined to learn all he could about Washington's unique military style, Lafayette proved to be a brilliant pupil, and Washington soon gave him a command of his own. Lafayette was a courageous officer, admired and respected both by his men and his superiors. His greatest service to the Revolution, however, would come later, and it would be political rather than military.

In May 1778 General Howe was recalled to London. He was replaced by his second-in-command, Sir Henry Clinton, whose orders were to evacuate Philadelphia, move his army to New York, and prepare to repel a French invasion. The Redcoats began their trek to the north in mid-June. Marching through New Jersey on a parallel course, waiting for the right moment to attack, was Washington's army.

Washington decided that the moment had arrived on the blisteringly hot morning of June 28. The evening before, he had sent half his army, under

America owes a great deal to General Washington for this day's work. A general rout, dismay, and disgrace would have attended the army in any other hands but his.
—ALEXANDER HAMILTON
American patriot, on
Washington's leadership at
the Battle of Monmouth

the command of General Charles Lee, to a position six miles away from Clinton's army, camped near the New Jersey town of Monmouth Court House. Lee's orders were to attack at first light. Washington, with the rest of the army, would immediately follow up with support.

The British troops, staggering in the sun under the weight of heavy uniforms and bulky packs, should have been easy marks. But as Washington confidently approached the scene of the attack, he was met by an amazing sight. Wave after wave of Lee's troops were heading toward him, racing to the rear in panicked retreat.

Lee, a frequent critic of Washington, had opposed the attack plan from the start. When Washington learned that Lee had reacted to the first sign of British resistance by ordering a retreat, the general was almost beside himself with fury. According to some reports, he let loose a string of oaths about Lee that impressed even his battle-toughened troops. His only officially recorded remark, however, was "Damn him!"

Not satisfied with putting Lee's regiments to flight, the British had decided to counterattack and were now charging down on the milling, disorga-

"Molly Pitcher" stokes cannon at the Battle of Monmouth. The wife of an artillery captain, Mary Hays had earned her nickname by carrying pitchers of water to wounded soldiers. She followed her husband onto the battlefield; when he was wounded, she coolly continued to fire his cannon until the battle ended.

nized Americans. Washington quickly reorganized his men, who — thanks in large part to the training they had received from Steuben — responded with crisp efficiency. The general, highly visible on his great horse, seemed to be everywhere at once. Lafayette later wrote that "with one glance," Washington had created order out of chaos. "I thought then as now," said the admiring Frenchman, "that I had never beheld so superb a man."

By nightfall the Americans had driven the British back to a defensive position. Washington allowed his exhausted troops to rest, planning to renew his attack at dawn. He was, however, denied the victory he hungered for: when the sun rose the next day, there was no sign of the Redcoats. Clinton, who evidently had no wish to meet the surprisingly strong American forces again, had marched his men away during the night. The Battle of Monmouth Court House — thanks in large part to Charles Lee's failure to obey Washington's orders — had ended as a draw. Lee was later court-martialed and dismissed from the army.

Washington had a relatively quiet year after the battle at Monmouth. Clinton and his army were snugly barricaded behind their fortifications in New York City, waiting to do battle with the incoming French fleet. Washington, who had established a sprawling base camp along the banks of the Hudson River outside New York, was also waiting for the French. He counted on them to make a substantial contribution to the Revolutionary forces.

Commanded by Count Jean-Baptiste d'Estaing, the French squadron arrived in New York in the summer of 1778. It was, however, to prove disappointing to both Clinton and Washington. At the sight of the heavily armed British navy at anchor in the harbor, d'Estaing sailed off, eventually arriving in the French West Indies, far from the American war. Such great expectations; such fizzled hopes!

There were other problems, too. The French had brought ships and soldiers to America, but Washington soon found that coordinating action between his own forces and those of the French was difficult. French ships were often not where Washington

American General Benedict Arnold passes secret papers to British spy John André. Arnold, a brilliant officer and close friend of Washington, had decided to sell out to the enemy after being repeatedly passed over for promotion. His name has become a synonym for "traitor."

wanted or expected them to be; the language barrier presented problems; French officers were sometimes reluctant to take orders from Americans. Many Americans, remembering their recent war with the French, were in turn highly suspicious of their new allies.

In public, Washington was the soul of diplomacy, doing his best to smooth out the ragged relationship between his countrymen and Lafayette's. Privately, however, he was frequently exasperated by the patronizing attitude of the French toward the less sophisticated Americans. "I most devoutly wish," he said in a letter to a friend, "that we had not a single foreign officer among us except the Marquis of Lafayette."

Meanwhile, the war dragged on. The British, whose extensive navy gave them almost complete control of America's coastal waters, mounted a seaborne invasion of Georgia in late 1778; by the following spring, a royal governor was seated in Savannah and the British flag was flying over the statehouse.

Next, a British expedition marched on Charleston, South Carolina. Aided by Tories (colonists still loyal to the king) and a band of Cherokee Indians, the British forces ripped through the countryside, looting, burning, and indiscriminately killing civilians and soldiers alike. Charleston was saved at the last minute by a mounted unit led by Casimir Pulaski, a Polish cavalry officer who, like Lafayette, had come to America to fight for the revolutionaries. Soon after his dramatic rescue of Charleston, the 32-year-old Pulaski was killed during an assault on British-held Savannah.

The British now developed a new strategy: they would conquer the South and use it as a springboard from which to attack the rest of the American states. Charleston was essential to this plan, and the British were determined to take it. In mid-April 1780, a 14,000-man force from New York, led by General Henry Clinton and his second-in-command, General Charles Cornwallis, swept into the city's harbor. Backed up by 14 warships, the British force easily overwhelmed the American defenders,

I have been told that [Washington] preserves in battle the character of humanity which makes him so dear to his soldiers in camp.
—FRANÇOIS DE BARBE-MARBOIS
French politician

who surrendered on May 12. The fall of Charleston, after which the British took 5,500 prisoners, has been called the worst American defeat of the war.

When Clinton returned to New York, Cornwallis was left in command of the British campaign in the South. Moving quickly, he won battle after battle; in three months, most of South Carolina was under the British flag. Cornwallis's victories depended heavily on units, or "legions," of Tory soldiers.

Most notorious of these legions was the one led by Banastre Tarleton, a British officer whose nickname — "Bloody" — suited him well. Among Tarleton's more notable forays was the "Waxhaws Massacre," which took place near the border of North Carolina in May 1780. After an outnumbered band of Virginia militia had surrendered to Tarleton, he and his men slaughtered 113 prisoners, savagely slashing the remaining 150 men with bayonets. (A horrified witness to the scene was a little boy named Andrew Jackson, who vowed he would someday avenge the massacre. Before he became president of the United States in 1828, Jackson would deliver a sound blow to his old enemy at the Battle of New Orleans in 1815.)

These were dark days for the revolutionaries. In a fierce battle at Camden, South Carolina, in August 1780, Cornwallis routed an army led by General Horatio Gates. The following September an American patrol halted a suspiciously nervous traveler in Tarrytown, New York. He was dressed as a civilian, but papers discovered in one of his boots told a different story: he was Major John André of the British army, and he was carrying detailed drawings of West Point, a vital American fortress on the Hudson River. The classified information on West Point was in the handwriting of Benedict Arnold.

Arnold was not only a trusted general, but Washington's close friend. The commander in chief, unaware of Arnold's growing bitterness following his unsung victory at Saratoga, was stunned. "Arnold has betrayed us!" he said. "Whom can we trust now?" Arnold escaped to a British warship after his treasonous act had been discovered. André was tried by a military court and sentenced to death.

The British pleaded for their man's life, but Washington refused to let him go unless Arnold was returned, and this the British refused to do. On October 2 André was hanged. Arnold became a brigadier general in the British army, later conducting raids on American towns.

"Traitors are the growth of every country," wrote a saddened Washington, "and in a revolution of the present nature, it is more to be wondered at" that the number is "so small." Washington felt, as he said a few months later, "at the end of his tether." Would the conflict ever end? Would he ever be able to turn the tide to America's advantage? Would he see again the Virginia hills and his plantation on the Potomac?

In January 1781 "Bloody" Tarleton's legion lost a major battle to the American army at Cowpens, South Carolina, but two months later, Cornwallis defeated the Americans at Guilford Court House, near present-day Greensboro, North Carolina. The British drive was still on.

In April Cornwallis moved north, invading Virginia. Tarleton advanced as far as Charlottesville, where his troops almost captured Governor Thomas Jefferson at his Monticello home. Cornwallis was winning battles, but his victories were bought at the cost of very heavy casualties, and his military strength was gradually weakening. Also working against him was the rising tide of local resistance generated by the brutality of his troops. Americans in the South were beginning to rally against the despised invader.

In late July Cornwallis moved the bulk of his forces to Yorktown, Virginia, where he started building a vast military and naval base. Meanwhile, in the North, Washington was preparing an offensive. On an earlier voyage to his homeland, the dedicated Lafayette had performed what was perhaps his greatest service to the American cause: he had persuaded King Louis XVI to send troops, ships, and supplies to aid the revolutionaries.

Part of Louis's contribution was a 6,700-man army under the command of Count de Rochambeau; part of it was a fleet of battleships commanded

THE BETTMANN ARCHIVE

Washington ignites the fuse of a cannon, symbolically opening the Battle of Yorktown. Eight days later, on October 17, 1781, General Charles Cornwallis, commander of the British forces in America, surrendered. Mopping-up operations remained, but the American Revolution was over.

The text in the cartoon reads:

liberty

Dear Mama say no more about it.

Be a good Girl and give me a Buss

George for Ever.

This British editorial cartoon, published in 1782, was captioned "The Reconciliation Between Britannia and Her Daughter America." Before Uncle Sam was created during the War of 1812, cartoonists often pictured the United States as an Indian, a snake, or an eagle.

by Admiral François de Grasse. Combining his own 5,000 troops with the French forces, Washington set out to trap Cornwallis in Yorktown.

Washington's plan was both simple and brilliant. His armies would march south, join the army headed by Lafayette in Virginia, and strike Cornwallis at Yorktown. At the same time the French fleet would sail into Chesapeake Bay, blocking any escape for the British. At last, the antagonism between the American and French allies disappeared; the two sides now worked together as a mighty and united force.

Washington's first move was to set up an elaborate ruse to deceive General Clinton in New York. He set up dummy camps in New Jersey and arranged for his spies to plant the false news that he was planning to attack New York. The plan worked perfectly;

intent on defending his position, Clinton stayed put, and sent no troops to assist Cornwallis.

Into Pennsylvania and Maryland marched Washington's and Rochambeau's troops. In early September 1781, the army's dusty columns arrived in Virginia. Their general was finally back on his own home ground. Arriving from the West Indies with 3,000 Frenchmen, Admiral de Grasse blocked the mouth of Chesapeake Bay. Cornwallis was rapidly being enclosed in a vise.

Washington now commanded an army of 17,000 men, well supplied with artillery. Cornwallis had less than half that number. On October 9 Washington ceremoniously touched a match to a cannon, starting the battle. As the American and French bombardment began and British defenses began to crumble, Cornwallis knew he was beaten. On October 17, 1781, he raised the flag of surrender.

The October 19 ceremony marking Cornwallis's defeat was an extraordinary moment in the history of America and in the life of George Washington. As columns of American and French soldiers lined up

Washington bids an emotional farewell to his officers at New York City's Fraunces Tavern on December 4, 1783. "Such a scene of sorrow and weeping," wrote one observer, "I had never before witnessed." Outside, a huge crowd was waiting to say its own goodbye to the American hero.

to receive them, regiment after regiment of Redcoats marched forward and laid down their arms, finally presenting Cornwallis's sword. The British military band played a tune whose message was clear. It was called "The World Turned Upside Down."

It had been six grueling years since Washington had taken over a disorganized, ragged group of soldiers in Boston, years in which defeat had often seemed certain. But now, here in Virginia, where he had spent most of his lifetime, where decades ago he had begun his military career, he savored a moment of supreme triumph.

The Battle of Yorktown was not the last military action in the war, but it signaled American victory. The British government was now ready to begin peace negotiations. In France, American negotiators John Adams, Benjamin Franklin, and John Jay met with the British to hammer out the terms of the Treaty of Paris, which recognized the United States of America as "free, sovereign, and independent." This document, finally signed on September 3, 1783, defined the new nation's territories as stretching from the Atlantic seaboard to the Mississippi River, from the Great Lakes to Florida. Benjamin Franklin summed it up: "We are now," he said, "friends with England and with all mankind."

At Fraunces Tavern in New York, George Washington held a final meeting with his officers on December 4, 1783. He was 51 years old. The chestnut-haired planter of 1775 had turned gray during the war; he now wore glasses to read. But the impressive bearing, the image that spoke of leadership and trust, were unchanged. He spoke only a few words that day, his eyes misting with emotion.

"With a heart full of love and gratitude, I now take leave of you," he said. "I most devoutly wish that your later days may be as prosperous and happy as your former ones have been glorious and honorable. . . . I shall feel obliged if each of you will come and take me by the hand." Led by hulking Henry Knox, the officers, themselves weeping, threw their arms around the man with whom they had suffered and endured so much.

Washington now headed south toward Virginia.

Guard against the impostures of pretended patriotism.
—GEORGE WASHINGTON

As he rode across New Jersey into Pennsylvania, he passed places he would never forget: Trenton, the Delaware River, Germantown, Brandywine. In every town along his route, people cheered, guns boomed, and church bells rang out, celebrating George Washington and American independence.

On December 23, 1783, Washington met with the Continental Congress in Annapolis, Maryland. He was resigning his commission as commander of the army. This moment in Washington's life deeply impressed not only his fellow Americans but also leaders in Europe. Washington was voluntarily giving up his military power.

"Having now finished the work assigned me," he declared to the Congress, "I retire from the great theater of action; and bidding an affectionate farewell to this august body under whose orders I have so long acted, I here offer my commission, and take my leave of all the employments of public life."

And so it was back to Mount Vernon, back to the life Washington loved above all else. It somehow seemed fitting that it was Christmas Eve when the retired general once again walked through the door of his mansion on the Potomac.

Mount Vernon's tranquil acres exerted a constant pull on George Washington. When the Revolution ended at last, he returned to the plantation gratefully, convinced that he would spend the rest of his days there in peaceful retirement. Subsequent events proved him a better general than prophet.

PATRIÆ PATE

7

From Planter to President

In 1783 Washington was — as he happily remarked to Lafayette — "a private citizen on the banks of the Potomac, and under the shadow of my own vine and my own fig tree." Deeply absorbed in the management of his plantation, he experimented with the latest methods of restoring depleted soil, tried new seeds, constructed modern barns. He enjoyed it all. "I think," he wrote, "that the life of a husbandman [farmer] is honorable. It is amusing, and with judicious management, it is profitable."

The master of Mount Vernon could now stand peacefully on his porch, observing the Potomac flowing below him, the gently rolling hills in the distance. In the mornings he could ride out to fields called Muddy Hole and Dogue Run, talk to his workers, oversee the planting of wheat and rye and Irish potatoes. Yes, he thought, this was the "most delectable" of lives. His dream of an uninterrupted existence in his rural paradise, however, was not to last for very long.

Mount Vernon soon became a haven for visitors ranging from Washington's old war acquaintances

The Revolution of the United States was the result of a mature and reflecting preference for freedom, not of a vague or ill-defined craving for independence.
—ALEXIS DE TOCQUEVILLE
19th-century French
author and statesman

Washington, whose prestige among his countrymen was enormous, was known as "the Father of his Country" (*Patriae Pater*) even before America's victory in the Revolution. Wherever he went, he was followed by crowds eager to see him, to hear his voice, and, as one observer put it, "to get a touch of him."

THE BETTMANN ARCHIVE

to foreign dignitaries. As a southern gentleman was expected to do, Washington gracefully welcomed the stream of people who made their way to his plantation. He became, in fact, something of a permanent host. In June 1785 he noted in his diary, "Dined with only Mrs. Washington, which I believe is the first instance of it since my retirement from public life."

Then there were the letters. They rained in on Mount Vernon from all over the world, some from friends, many from people he did not know. They asked for his opinions, his political advice, his money. There was so much mail that he began, he said, "to feel the weight and oppression of it." He dutifully answered most of the correspondence, but he refused even to consider appeals that he accept public office — although any office in the government could have been his for the asking.

Since 1781 the American government had operated under the Articles of Confederation, a loose "league of friendship." Under the Articles, the central government — Congress — had the power to conduct foreign relations and issue money, but the individual states retained the power to tax, regulate trade, and raise troops. There was no central executive officer, or president, of the nation.

After the war was over, Congress found itself trying to function with almost no money. The nation's fiscal system was on the brink of chaos. Inflation was rampant. A pound of tea for example, cost $100 in some parts of the country. (By comparison, an army private's salary was $4 per month.) The nation's depressed economy was taking its toll on many small farmers. Some were being thrown in jail for debt and many were forced to watch their farms being sold at auction.

In 1786 some of the farmers, led by former Continental Army Captain Daniel Shays, fought back. Determined to prevent the circuit court at Northampton, Massachusetts, from foreclosing on their farms, they threatened to seize the thousands of muskets stored in the Continental Army arsenal at Springfield. Although Shays' Rebellion, as the insurrection was known, was put down by local mi-

THE BETTMANN ARCHIVE

Washington offers Nelson, his old war-horse, a lump of sugar at Mount Vernon. A superb horseman, Washington enjoyed nothing more than his daily canters around his vast estate.

litiamen, the incident confirmed the fears of many Americans that a complete breakdown of authority was just around the corner, and that the government lacked the power to control it.

Washington had already come to believe that the government under the Articles of Confederation was a "rope of sand," incapable of maintaining order. He was shocked by Shays' Rebellion, which he saw as further evidence that the government needed to be revised, needed to be given enough power to deal with such emergencies. "There are combustibles in every state which a spark might set fire to," he said. "I feel infinitely more than I can express for the disorders which have arisen. Good God!" It was time, said Washington, "to rescue the political machine from the impending storm."

Delegates from five states had met earlier in the year to discuss ways of improving the government. They had decided that the Articles of Confederation needed overhauling, and that all 13 states should be represented at their next meeting, which would be held in Philadelphia in May 1787.

At the time, no one expected the conference to produce much of great importance, and Washington's presence had not been demanded. Shays' Rebellion changed everything. Now the nation's influential men strongly urged the retired general to attend the conference as the leader of Virginia's delegation.

Washington relaxes at Mount Vernon with Martha and their two grandchildren, adopted by the Washingtons after the death of Martha's son, Jacky Custis. Although Washington had hoped to remain aloof from public affairs after the Revolution, such peaceful moments at home were rare.

Washington, however, was inclined to leave the task of revising the government to such men as James Madison. Madison was ready. The Philadelphia convention, he believed, would provide the perfect opportunity to frame a new government. Washington was unsure. Although he believed in establishing a stronger government, was this the way to proceed? Would the American people accept the revision of the government by such a convention? Should revision be made through Congress itself or by some other means?

Suffering from rheumatism, absorbed in the management of Mount Vernon, Washington was plagued with doubts about whether he should attend the convention. He brooded about his decision and almost stayed home. But finally he agreed to go. Madison was enormously pleased. He knew that the general's mere presence would give the gathering an air of importance it might otherwise lack. With the participation of the illustrious Washington, the Philadelphia convention would draw the attention of the entire country.

Washington arrived in Philadelphia on May 13, 1787. Just as they had after the Revolution, the townspeople greeted him with thunderous cheers and the roar of cannon and muskets. He entered the city to the tolling of the Liberty Bell atop the Pennsylvania State House, the bell that had rung out after the signing of the Declaration of Independence more than a decade earlier.

As the 55 delegates gathered for the opening of the convention, Washington recognized a crowd of familiar faces. Many of those present had served as officers in the Continental Army; some, including Alexander Hamilton, had served on Washington's own staff.

Two of America's most important political figures, John Adams and Thomas Jefferson, were in Europe during the convention. Others, notably Patrick Henry, had refused to participate. (Henry, who said he "smelt a rat," feared that the convention was a plot to saddle the country with an oppressive central government much like the one it had so recently overthrown.)

An option is still left to the United States of America . . . whether they will be respectable and prosperous, or contemptible and miserable, as a nation. This is the time of their political probation.
—GEORGE WASHINGTON
on the U.S. government
under the Articles
of Confederation

Embattled farmers cheer as a supporter of Shays' Rebellion pummels an opponent in Northampton, Massachusetts. The 1786 uprising, led by Continental Army veteran Daniel Shays, was triggered by foreclosures of farms for unpaid taxes. American leaders were shaken by the rebellion, which suggested a collapse of national order.

Even without these important men, however, the convention featured an impressive cast of political leaders and thinkers — James Madison, Benjamin Franklin, Alexander Hamilton, George Mason, John Dickinson, Gouverneur Morris, and many others. Most of the delegates had studied law, had served in colonial or state legislatures, or had been members of Congress.

Philadelphia was in the grip of a fierce heat wave, and on May 25, 1787, the city was sweltering. The cobblestoned street in front of the Pennsylvania State House was covered with a fresh layer of dirt to muffle the sound of passing carriages and carts. Inside, Robert Morris of Pennsylvania opened the proceedings with a nomination — George Washington for the presidency of the convention. He was unanimously elected. Characteristically, he said he was not qualified for such a great office, but each of the men present knew the Virginian's leadership would be essential in the days to come.

The delegates to the convention disagreed about many things, but they were united on one point: the necessity for a new constitution, not merely a revised version of the Articles of Confederation. In the beginning, however, it seemed that the delegates' points of difference would outweigh their common aims. Representatives from Virginia and

He has a dignity which forbids familiarity, mixed with an easy affability which creates love and reverence.
—ABIGAIL ADAMS
American writer and wife of U.S. President John Adams, on Washington

The Liberty Bell atop Philadelphia's Independence Hall had been rung to celebrate the signing of the Declaration of Independence in 1776. Hidden during the Revolution, the great bell was remounted after the war; its joyous peals greeted Washington's 1787 arrival in Philadelphia.

other large states wanted representation in the new government to be determined by population. The small states demanded an equal voice for each state. Some members were especially hostile to the idea of a strong chief executive.

During an adjournment of the meetings, Washington and Gouverneur Morris decided to refresh their spirits with a ride through the countryside. Their path led them to Valley Forge, where Washington and his troops had spent the bitter winter of 1777–78. While Morris cast for trout, Washington pensively looked over the now green hills where he had once wondered if the American Revolution was doomed. The country, he must have thought, had accomplished much. And it would accomplish still more in the months to come.

Back in session on August 6, the delegates set to work on the first draft of the Constitution. Hour after hour, week after week, they labored in the confines of the sultry convention hall. Through the long month of August the members made proposals and compromises; they argued and persuaded. They were, after all, creating a form of government that had never before existed.

Some of the delegates were so displeased by the proceedings that they walked out; others, such as Washington's fellow Virginia delegates, George Mason and Edmund Randolph, stayed to the end but refused to sign the final document.

By early September the final form of the Constitution was clear. It gave the federal government new authority, including the power to tax, regulate trade, and issue money. There would be a president of the United States, elected for a four-year term by an electoral college chosen by the people.

There would be a legislature consisting of two houses: the Senate, composed of two members from each state, and a House of Representatives in which the number of each state's members would depend on the state's population. And there would be a Supreme Court, whose members were to be appointed for life by the president.

A system of "checks and balances" among the government's three branches — the executive (the president), the legislative (the two houses of Congress), and the judicial (the Supreme Court) — would ensure that none of the branches would have greater power over the other.

On September 17, 1787, the weary convention delegates met for the last time. Although none of them was completely satisfied with the Constitution they had written, they knew they had done their best. How it would be received by the rest of the country, said Washington, "is not for me to decide, nor shall I say anything for or against it. If it be good, I suppose it will work its way good. If bad, it will recoil on the framers."

Benjamin Franklin sounded equally unsure of what the convention had wrought. He said he signed the Constitution "because I expect no better, and because I am not sure that it is not the best." The debate over the nation's form of government was now set for a larger arena. Before it became the

Independence Hall in Philadelphia was built betweeen 1732 and 1757. It was here that the Declaration of Independence, the Articles of Confederation, and the Constitution were signed. Washington called the convention that produced the Constitution "the miracle at Philadelphia."

Washington presides over the Constitutional Convention of 1787. The 55 delegates to the Philadelphia meeting were surprisingly young. Their average age was 42; five were still in their 20s, and four were under 35. At 55, Washington was one of the oldest.

Our Constitution is in actual operation; everything appears to promise that it will last; but nothing in this world is certain but death and taxes.

—BENJAMIN FRANKLIN
American patriot, in 1789

law of the land, the Constitution still had to be ratified, or approved, by at least 9 of the 13 states.

Washington rode home to Mount Vernon. The mansion, which its owner had been rebuilding and enlarging for years, was now almost finished. One of the final items to be fitted into place was a copper weathervane in the shape of a dove, which was placed at the very top of the building. Washington, one of the most famous generals in the world, had capped his home with a symbol of peace.

The ratification debates in the states were long and often bitter. In several state conventions the outcome remained in doubt for months. Opponents of the Constitution, who were now being called "Antifederalists," argued that the Philadelphia convention had exceeded its authority. They asserted that its members — most of whom were rich landowners — had secretly plotted to increase the power of the country's wealthy men. They pointed out that the document lacked a bill of rights guaranteeing such personal liberties as freedom of speech and freedom of religion.

The Constitution's supporters, the "Federalists," had a powerful advantage: the support of America's two most celebrated men, Benjamin Franklin and George Washington. The choice, said Washington, was between the Constitution and a nation no longer united. The Federalists finally won over their opponents, largely by promising to support a series of amendments to the Constitution that would provide a bill of rights. (True to their word, they guided through the First Congress legislation that became the Bill of Rights.)

In June 1788 New Hampshire finally voted for ratification, supplying the necessary ninth vote of approval. America's new government, based on the Constitution, was now legally established. The last holdouts — Virginia, New York, North Carolina, and Rhode Island — ratified soon afterward.

The next step for the infant country was the selection of a president. The choice was obvious. There was only one man universally respected and admired in every state, one man who symbolized the liberty so dearly bought on the battlefield, one man trusted by his countrymen to guide them into the future. George Washington was unanimously elected president of the United States of America on February 4, 1789.

To Washington, the task ahead seemed overwhelming. He compared it to "entering upon an unexplored field, enveloped on every side with clouds and darkness." True to his style, however, he once again left Mount Vernon, this time to serve his country in peace. He set out for New York City, now the national capital, on April 14, 1789.

En route to his inauguration ceremony in New York City on April 14, 1789, Washington says goodbye to his wife and grandchildren at Mount Vernon. Martha, distressed about reentering public life, declined to attend the ceremony. Washington himself said he departed with "anxious and painful sensations."

8

The First Administration

Washington's riotous welcome to New York — complete with flowers, banners and bands, newspaper tributes to "our adored leader," thundering cannon and clanging bells — was a genuine expression of the nation's affection for its new president.

Washington, however, was not eager to begin the awesome job to which he had been elected. He had often told friends that he preferred his private life at Mount Vernon, often expressed his dismay over political intrigue and squabbling, often said that he would accept public service only if duty required it. He told his friend Henry Knox that he approached the presidency with all the enthusiasm of a condemned man nearing the gallows.

Washington was even distressed by the public excitement that greeted his every appearance, fearing that his performance would disappoint his admirers. "So much is expected," he groaned, ". . . that I feel an insuperable diffidence in my own abilities." As the new government began its work, James Madison observed, "We are in a wilderness." And everyone depended on Washington to lead them out.

The administration of justice is the firmest pillar of government.
—GEORGE WASHINGTON

Washington (right) confers with his first cabinet. Its members included (from the left) Secretary of War Henry Knox, Secretary of State Thomas Jefferson, Attorney General Edmund Randolph, and Secretary of the Treasury Alexander Hamilton. Another Washington appointee was Supreme Court Chief Justice John Jay.

A wooden statuette of Washington, carved about 1825. The nation's first president was the subject of countless portraits and statues. His likeness was probably familiar to more people of his time than that of any other living individual.

Washington had some good reasons for being reluctant to assume the presidency. The new government's only inheritance from its days under the Articles of Confederation was a few clerks who were owed back wages, a huge national debt, no incoming taxes or the machinery to collect any, an army of 672 men, and no navy at all. Furthermore, the British still clung to their forts in the Northwest, and Spain was showing signs of wanting American land in the West.

Washington was not an expert in political theory or national finance or foreign affairs. He was, however, a forceful leader and a dogged, sensible administrator. He was determined to establish the new government on a sound footing. As the nation's first chief executive, he knew that every move he made would set an example for the country's future presidents.

Conscious of this immense responsibility, he worked hard to balance the conflicts that soon surfaced in the capital. The large states contended with the small ones; representatives of northern interests vied with those who argued for the needs of the South; members who represented commercial interests squared off against those representing agriculture.

Immersed as it was in debts, hampered by a shortage of skilled employees, beset by constant wrangling and bickering, the new government made surprising progress. Congress quickly passed the Bill of Rights, which was soon ratified by the states; it set up a federal court system and began to create a new financial structure.

Washington was blessed with a group of extraordinarily able men from which to choose his cabinet members. For secretary of state, he selected his fellow Virginian, Thomas Jefferson, who had demonstrated his diplomatic skills as minister to France. He named Alexander Hamilton of New York as treasury secretary; 34 years old, Hamilton was a financial wizard as well as an early and staunch supporter of the Constitution.

Washington's choice for secretary of war was Henry Knox, his old chief of artillery. John Jay of

New York, who had been secretary of foreign affairs under the Articles of Confederation, became the first chief justice of the Supreme Court.

The Constitution did not spell out all the details of the presidency. Although Washington asked that he be given no salary, Congress fixed the amount at $25,000 a year, a stupendous sum in 1789. It was clear that the president was expected to entertain in high style. His title was a matter for debate. A Senate committee suggested "His Highness, the President of the United States of America, and Protector of their Liberties," but the House of Representatives objected vehemently. Congress and Washington finally agreed on the form of address still in use: "Mr. President."

At times Washington did display an air of formality that irritated those who remembered with scorn the days when Americans were under the rule of a British king. At official functions the president often dressed in black velvet and satin, wore yellow gloves and diamond knee buckles, and carried a long sword. He drove around New York in a stately carriage pulled by six cream-colored horses.

In October 1789 Washington left New York for a month's tour of New England. The trip was to provide the president with both a vacation and a first-hand look at a part of the country he had known only as a series of battlegrounds. As his carriage bounced along the rough, pitted roads of Massachusetts and Connecticut, Washington kept a diary in which he made notes about commerce, shipping, seaports, and factories.

> *Although his every move could be deemed a potential precedent binding generations unborn, his foot did not slip once.*
> —THOMAS A. BAILEY
> American historian, on Washington's presidency

NATIONAL ARCHIVES

Manufactured in England, this coach was used by Washington and his family when they traveled out of Mount Vernon. Washington's presidential trips around the country were made in a similar vehicle.

He was apparently especially interested in a sail factory in Boston that was staffed largely by young women. Washington, who was known for his appreciation of "the fair sex," reported in his journal that he had congratulated the manager of the factory for hiring "the prettiest girls in Boston."

The following spring, Washington took a two-month, 1,900-mile journey through the South. Because communications between various parts of the country were slow and unreliable, he left instructions for any political or other emergencies that might arise while he was away from the capital.

Traveling in a most unroyal way, he was attended only by his carriage drivers and his manservant. In the evenings, the presidential party would stop, unannounced, at small country inns. "Innkeepers were amazed," writes historian James Flexner, "when a little cavalcade that had turned into their dooryards — a coach, a baggage wagon, and some led extra horses — proved to contain 'the greatest man in the world.' "

A gorgeously dressed admirer crowns Benjamin Franklin with a laurel wreath at a ball in Paris. The opulent lifestyle of Washington and his associates was not universally admired in the new American republic; it reminded some critics of the excesses of the prerevolutionary French court.

THE BETTMANN ARCHIVE

Washington's tours showed him that the nation was relatively prosperous, that it had accepted the government under the Constitution, and that his support as president was widespread. His travels also made him sharply aware of the astonishing diversity among the people, customs, and interests of the country. As the business of the new government progressed, it became clear that deep political divisions threatened the unity and stability Washington craved for his nation.

The principal division was between those — now known as Federalists — who favored a strong federal government and those who wanted the states to retain political supremacy. Members of this group, who had begun to call themselves Democratic-Republicans or simply Republicans, were often the same men who, as Antifederalists, had opposed the Constitution. As Republicans, however, they no longer objected to the Constitution; on the contrary, they insisted on its strict, literal interpretation. The Federalists were the predecessors of today's Republican party; the Republicans, of today's Democrats.

The Republicans and Federalists differed on the meaning of the Constitution, on state versus federal rights, even in appearance. While the Federalists continued to wear traditional knee breeches and powdered wigs, and to maintain old-fashioned, elegant manners, many Republicans adopted the styles current in France, where a revolution against the monarchy had begun in 1789. These admirers of the French radicals took to wearing short, unpowdered hair and baggy pants, and to addressing each other in the French revolutionary manner as "Citizen" or "Citizeness."

Washington, who continued to dress in the conventional fashion, was personally more sympathetic to the Federalists' philosophy than to that of the Republicans. He dreaded the idea of conflicting political parties, however, believing that their growth could destroy the fledgling nation. Determined to prevent political discord if humanly possible, he carefully avoided political quarrels, and kept partisans of both sides in his government.

> *Washington was the one truly "indispensable man." With his towering prestige, unfaltering leadership, and sterling character, he was perhaps the only man in the history of the presidency bigger than the government itself.*
> —THOMAS A. BAILEY
> American historian

Within his administration, the two factions fought like tigers. Much of the controversy surrounded proposals made by Alexander Hamilton, Washington's secretary of the treasury and the leader of the Federalists. A vigorous, articulate advocate of a strong central government, Hamilton distrusted the masses and favored increased federal authority to provide order and stability. He believed that the government should be controlled by people of wealth and education.

When Hamilton took over the Treasury Department, the government was saddled with massive Revolutionary War debts, which were owed both to foreign countries and American creditors. The individual states were also deeply in debt.

Hamilton insisted that the new federal government should pay off both the federal and state debts. He proposed to raise the money by taxing goods imported from other countries as well as those manufactured and sold in the United States. He also advocated the creation of a national bank, which would act as the government's depository and as a central authority controlling the operation of all state banks.

John Adams, the first U.S. ambassador to England, presents his credentials to George III in 1785. Although the British king agreed with Adams's hope for a restoration of "the old good nature and the old good humor," postwar diplomatic relations between the two countries were to prove far from smooth.

Hamilton was hotly opposed by Secretary of State Thomas Jefferson, who was the leader of the Republicans. Jefferson agreed that the debts owed by the federal government should be paid, but he strongly objected to the idea of national taxation to pay state debts.

He argued that such taxes would be an intolerable burden on farmers, tradesmen, and other middle- and lower-class Americans. Jefferson asserted that Hamilton's system would make government the oppressor of its people. It would, he said, burden the country with a tyranny no less vicious than the one America had so recently overthrown.

Jefferson and his political ally, James Madison (who was then a member of the House of Representatives), also vehemently opposed Hamilton's plan for a national bank. They maintained that such a bank was both unnecessary and unconstitutional, and they urged Washington to veto the bill that would create it.

Washington wanted, above all, a government that could act swiftly and decisively, one that could bind the nation together by promoting commerce and industry. In the end, Hamilton convinced him that a national bank was in the country's best interests, and was not contrary to the Constitution; Washington signed the bill. Hamilton also succeeded in his campaign to have the federal government assume the states' war debts.

Washington despaired over the deepening, seething political quarrels. Appalled by the "warmth and intemperance" with which each side attacked the other, he was particularly distressed by the deteriorating relationship between his two most important cabinet members.

Jefferson and Hamilton's mutual antagonism had grown sharper, and they no longer concealed their hatred of one another. Jefferson called his rival the "bastard brat of a Scots peddler" (Hamilton was an illegitimate child); Hamilton said Jefferson was a "contemptible hypocrite" whose politics were "tinged with fanaticism."

Even at elegant social functions, Washington

Thomas Jefferson, Washington's secretary of state and the third president of the United States, was a brilliant writer, philosopher, and politician. He was, however, an unhappy ally for Washington, with whom he disagreed on most important issues.

MOUNT VERNON LADIES ASSOCIATION

Washington crowned his Mount Vernon mansion with a dove of peace. If the nations of the world concentrated on "philanthropy, industry, and economy" instead of on "war, bloodshed, and desolation," he said in a letter to a friend, "how much happier would mankind be!"

heard bitter and impassioned speeches; he saw old friends divided by politics; he heard of dignified officials brawling in taverns, on the streets, even in Congress itself.

But he persevered, trying to heal the political wounds between the two sides, trying to steer the government in what he saw as a reasonable, appropriate course. In 1792 he sent letters to Jefferson and Hamilton, saying almost the same words to each man. "How unfortunate," he wrote, "that internal dissensions should be harrowing and tearing our vitals. Without more charity . . . the fairest prospect of happiness and prosperity that was ever presented to man will be lost."

Washington was exhausted by the nonstop political battles raging about him, and he was depressed by his inability to enforce harmony in his administration. He was resentful of the mudslinging that had begun to involve him directly, and horrified by the thought that, despite his efforts, the nation might fly apart into warring regions.

He began to talk seriously about retiring when his term was over in the spring of 1793. James Madison reported that Washington had told him he would rather "go to his farm, take his spade in his hand, and work for his bread" than serve another term.

The major combatants in the political war — Jefferson, Hamilton, and Madison — finally had something they could agree on. Shocked by the thought of Washington's departure, they joined forces and implored him to stay on. He alone, they said, stood above partisan politics; he alone could work with both sides. "The confidence of the whole union is centered on you," declared Jefferson to his chief. "North and South will hang together, if they have you to hang on."

Washington finally agreed to allow his name to be placed in nomination for a second term. When Congress tabulated the Electoral College votes in February 1793, it found that Washington — as expected — had been unanimously reelected. On March 4, 1793, he and his vice-president, John Adams, were once again sworn into office. Mount Vernon would have to wait.

Alexander Hamilton in the uniform of a New York Artillery Company officer in 1776. Hamilton, who served as Washington's personal aide from 1777 to 1781, became the first U.S. treasury secretary. A financial genius, he established the nation's fiscal system.

9

Challenges Foreign and Domestic

Two weeks after Washington began his second presidential term, echoes of conflict came rumbling across the Atlantic Ocean. On March 17, 1793, news arrived in the United States that delighted some Americans and horrified others: the king and queen of France, Louis XVI and Marie Antoinette, had been beheaded. France had declared itself a republic.

Washington believed that America's neutrality was essential to its survival. He was now faced with an enormous diplomatic problem: should he, or should he not, recognize the new French regime? The Republicans, led by Secretary of State Jefferson, had long been deeply sympathetic to the French revolutionaries, and they urged the president to recognize the new republic at once.

The Federalists, however, were sickened by the wave of bloody violence that had accompanied the French Revolution. They were also mindful of the invaluable assistance Louis had given the American Revolution, and they were outraged at the thought of America's recognition of the new regime.

Washington weighed the arguments on both sides. Then he officially recognized the French Re-

Kings, aristocrats, and tyrants, whoever they may be, are slaves in rebellion against the sovereign of the earth, which is mankind, and against the legislator of the universe, which is nature.
—MAXIMILIEN DE ROBESPIERRE
French revolutionary

Washington's natural dignity was accentuated by the black velvet suits he favored during his presidency. In any costume, however, he was an impressive figure. Well over six feet tall, he had steady, gray-blue eyes, a massive physique, and a regal bearing; he stood, reported one observer, "straight as an Indian."

THE BETTMANN ARCHIVE

L'Egalité (equality), symbol of the French Revolution, displays the Declaration of the Rights of Man. This document, which stated that "men are born free and equal in rights," was modeled after the American Declaration of Independence.

public. "We surely cannot deny to any nation," he said, "the right whereon our own government is founded, that every nation may govern itself according to whatever form it pleases." The Republicans were overjoyed, but their cheers turned to shouts of outrage after Washington's next move.

On April 22 he issued a proclamation of neutrality, which made American participation in the affairs of a foreign country illegal. The proclamation was unpopular with many Americans who felt that the French Revolution was a mirror of their own. Indeed, France's Declaration of the Rights of Man was similar in many respects to America's own Declaration of Independence. The American Francophiles (supporters of France) felt it was their country's duty to assist its French cousins.

France had not only turned itself into a republic, it had once again gone to war with its ancient enemy, Britain. The renewal of the seemingly endless French-British struggle presented Washington with another, even graver problem. The French and British war, he knew, could deeply involve the United States.

While there were many Francophiles in the United States, there was also a large body of Anglophiles — those whose sympathies lay with the British. This group, whose most influential member was Treasury Secretary Alexander Hamilton, detested the excesses of the French Revolution. They believed that the heritage of language and custom shared by Britain and the United States far outweighed any past associations with the French. In a letter to a British diplomat in New York, Hamilton said, "I have always preferred a connection with you [Britain] to that of any other country; *we think in English* and have a similarity of prejudices and predilections." The Anglophiles were also quick to point out that Britain was America's most important trading partner; the young nation, they insisted, could not afford to endanger its good relationship with Britain.

The United States was therefore divided into two camps: the Republican Francophiles, whose spokesman was Jefferson, and the Federalist Anglophiles, led by Hamilton. Washington himself continued to insist that the United States maintain strict neutrality. At the same time, he confirmed his country's recognition of the new French government by preparing to receive its minister, "Citizen" Edmond Genêt.

A flamboyant and energetic young revolutionary, Genêt had been sent to the United States to obtain American assistance for France. When he learned of Washington's declaration of neutrality, he was appalled. How could the United States turn its back on France, the country that had enabled the Americans to win their own revolution? How could Washington betray his principal ally?

When he arrived in the United States in the spring of 1793, Genêt did not immediately arrange to meet Washington, as diplomatic practice demanded. Instead, he scurried around the country, commissioning American ships to attack the British, organizing pro-French clubs, and stirring up demonstrations against Washington and his neutrality policy. The president was amazed and infuriated, but his displeasure bothered the self-confident Frenchman not at all. "Old man Washington," he wrote to friends in Paris, "can't forgive my success."

Genêt called Washington a dupe of the British, a shadow of the man who had once fought the damnable Redcoats. Some excited Francophiles even suggested that perhaps Washington deserved the same fate as Louis XVI. Washington, for the first time in his life, was feeling the sting of vicious political invective aimed directly at himself.

When Genêt finally met with the president, Washington told him coldly that his actions were intolerable. Genêt ignored the hint, and at last, even the passionately pro-French Jefferson agreed that the United States should demand Genêt's recall. By then, however, Genêt's revolutionary faction had lost power in France; if he went home, he would follow Louis to the guillotine.

Genêt had sorely tried Washington's patience, but the president was a generous man. He permitted the young emissary to stay in America; Genêt married an American and settled down to the life of a New York farmer.

The rights of man in society are liberty, equality, security, and property.
—from France's "Declaration of the Rights of Man," 1795

The ambassador of revolutionary France, "Citizen" Edmond Genêt, introduces himself to Washington. By this time, Genêt's outspoken efforts to rally neutral America to the French cause had earned him the intense dislike of the president.

Meanwhile, the powerful British navy had begun to seize neutral ships — including American merchant vessels — that were trading with the French. More than 300 U.S. ships were captured; many of their sailors were forced to serve in the British navy. The anti-British feeling aroused by these acts of high-seas piracy was intensified by the continued British refusal to abandon their heavily armed forts in America's Ohio Valley. A new wave of Indian attacks on settlers in the area was being encouraged and aided by the British occupying the forts.

American rage against Britain now brought calls for war. Given the fact that the Americans had virtually no army or navy, such a prospect was unrealistic, but early in 1794 the United States did pass an embargo against all British shipping in American ports.

The embargo forced the British to decrease their hostile actions toward America's merchant vessels, and Washington decided to push for further gains. On May 12 he sent Chief Justice John Jay to London. Jay's mission was to negotiate a treaty obligating the British to withdraw from the Ohio forts and to pay for the American ships they had seized.

Washington, already deeply worried by foreign affairs, was now hit with a domestic crisis. Trouble was brewing in Pennsylvania. Farmers in that state had long depended on the money they made from selling whiskey, which they distilled from their surplus corn crops. They bitterly resented the tax the government had levied on whiskey distilling, and in July 1794 a group of them rebelled.

Refusing to pay the tax, the angry whiskey makers attacked both tax collectors and farmers who obeyed the law and paid their taxes. At a large rally in Pittsburgh, the tax rebels urged a full-scale revolt against the government. After several federal tax offices had been destroyed by mobs, Washington decided it was time to prove that the government was able to enforce its laws.

At the head of an army of 15,000 men, Washington rode from Philadelphia (which had been reestablished as the capital in 1790) into western

French guillotine operators demonstrate their grisly art. The execution machine was introduced in 1789 by J. J. Guillotin, a French physician, who praised its "humanitarian" qualities. Between June 1793 and July 1794, 17,000 French men and women lost their heads to the device's heavy blade.

Pennsylvania. The rebels fled at the sight of the president and his troops. The rebellion was over, and the farmers began paying their taxes. Washington had proved that federal law must be obeyed.

The Federalists strongly approved of Washington's forceful action against the Whiskey Rebellion, which Hamilton had called "treason against society." Thomas Jefferson and the Republicans, however, saw the move as a ruthless attack on lower-class citizens who were demonstrating against a real grievance, the unfair tax system. Jefferson called the action "an armament against people and their ploughs."

The Whiskey Rebellion weakened the Republicans' faith in the Washington administration, but the document that John Jay brought back from England in 1795 almost destroyed it. Jay's Treaty left unsettled the question of British repayment for seized American ships. It did contain Britain's as-

Vermonters cheer as their state, the 14th to join the Union, becomes part of the United States on March 4, 1791. Vermont, whose territory had long been claimed by New York, declared its independence in 1777; it elected a governor in 1778 and remained independent until it was admitted to the Union 13 years later.

surance that it would evacuate the Ohio Valley forts, but it also permitted the British to continue their fur trade with the Indians of the area. Since most of these tribes were extremely hostile to American settlers, this provision enraged the public.

Washington was not pleased with the document, but he considered it better than no treaty at all, and he sent it to the Senate for a vote. Its passage (by a very narrow vote) provoked months of furious public demonstrations across the nation. A sign chalked on a Boston wall read: "Damn John Jay! Damn everyone who won't damn John Jay!! Damn everyone who won't sit up all night damning John Jay!!!"

Maintaining U.S. neutrality in the British-French conflict was a difficult balancing act. It pleased neither political side, but Washington kept at it doggedly. He later said that his chief motive for keeping the United States out of the war had been "to gain time for our country to settle and mature." Before the nation could "command its own fortune," said Washington, it needed to develop "strength and consistency."

By the end of his second administration, Washington could see signs of national progress and prosperity. A 1796 treaty with Spain had given the United States the right to navigate freely in the Spanish-controlled Mississippi River "in its whole length from its source to the ocean." It also gave the United States free use of the port of New Orleans. A decisive victory over a confederation of Indians by American troops commanded by Anthony Wayne in the Ohio Valley had brought additional security to the northwestern frontier. Three new states — Vermont, Kentucky, and Tennessee — had joined the Union. New roads were under construction across the country. And a city on the Potomac River, just north of Mount Vernon, was being laid out. The future seat of the national government, it would be named for the country's first president.

Washington turned a deaf ear to all those who urged him to run for a third term. He knew he could be reelected easily, but he had no intention of proving it. The call of Mount Vernon would no longer be resisted; he was going home.

He is next only to the divinity.
—LORD BYRON
English poet,
on Washington

Washington's successor, John Adams, was an expert in political science but he lacked his predecessor's taste for administrative duties. Washington was away from the capital for 181 days during his eight years as president; Adams, who served four years, was absent from the seat of government for 385 days.

In September 1796 Washington published a farewell address to the American people. In it, he advised his fellow citizens to forget their regional differences, and to take pride in "the name of AMERICAN, which belongs to you." He said Americans should "observe good faith and justice toward all nations," but to have with those nations "as little *political* connection as possible." He counseled his countrymen to "steer clear of permanent alliances" and to "trust to temporary alliances for extraordinary emergencies."

The presidential election of 1796 pitted Federalist John Adams against Republican Thomas Jefferson. Adams won; Jefferson, because he had received the second highest number of votes, became vice-president. On March 4, 1797, Washington turned the presidency over to his successor.

Although Adams, as the nation's new president, had center stage, the eyes of most of those attending the inauguration ceremony in Philadelphia were on the tall, black-clad figure of George Washington. The

If we must rank presidents, Washington, in my judgment, deserves the place at the very top.

—THOMAS A. BAILEY
American historian

general's face, reported Adams in a letter to his wife Abigail, "was as serene and unclouded as the day." Apparently reading Washington's mind, Adams added, "Methought I heard him say, 'Ay, I'm fairly out and you're fairly in. See which of us will be happiest!' "

After the ceremony, Washington went to Adams's hotel to pay his respects. As he entered the door, he stopped and looked back at the immense crowd that had followed him. "And when he went inside at last," Adams wrote, "a great common voice went through the throng, as if they sobbed to see their hero go from their sight forever."

An early map of Washington, D.C., which became the nation's capital in 1800. The site had been chosen in 1790 by Washington, who also selected its architect, a Frenchman named Pierre L'Enfant. Jefferson, himself an architect, detested L'Enfant's plan, but it has since been hailed as a masterpiece of city design.

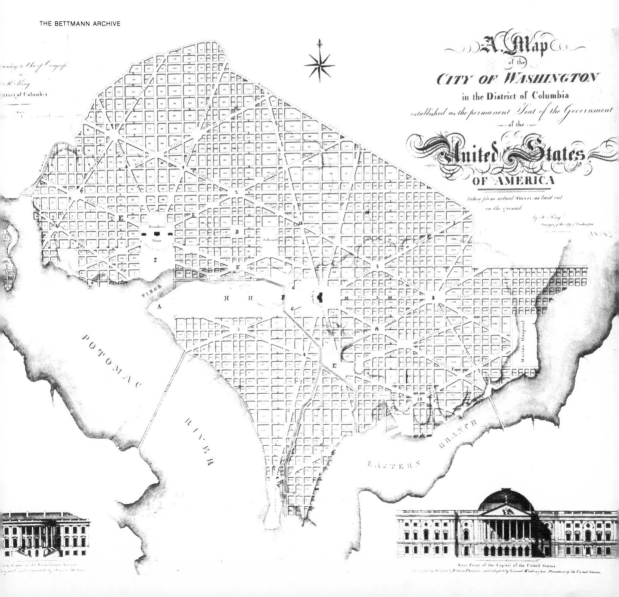

10

Citizen in Retirement

"I had rather be at Mount Vernon with a friend or two about me," Washington had written during his presidency, "than to be attended at the seat of government by the officers of state and the representatives of every power in Europe. . . ." He was glad to leave Philadelphia and the presidency. He had served his country long and faithfully, and now the burden of responsibility would be carried by others.

Before they left for Mount Vernon, the Washingtons sold much of the furniture they had used in their official residence. Still, moving the family's pets, wardrobes, and crates of household goods, along with Washington's large collection of paintings, was a major undertaking. Washington observed the confusion of moving day with humor. "On one side," he wrote, "I am called upon to remember the parrot; on the other, to remember the dog." As far as he was concerned, he added, "I should not pine if they were both forgot."

Washington found Mount Vernon in bad shape. In his long absence, the plantation had been neglected; the house needed major repairs; his once "scientifically" tended croplands were eroded and almost bare, and his livestock was puny and sharply reduced in number. He hired a small army of work-

NATIONAL ARCHIVES

Washington's desk and chair. When he left office, Washington sold much of his furniture to a woman friend. She later told him that a secret drawer in one of the pieces contained love letters. Only after much teasing did she reveal the identity of the letter writer: it was Martha Washington.

Washington posed for his last portrait in Philadelphia, where he was raising an army to defend the United States against a threatened French invasion. The likeness, drawn in crayon, was made in November 1798; 13 months later, George Washington was dead.

NEW YORK PUBLIC LIBRARY

men and immediately began to repair the "wounds" in his property.

Washington was 65 years old when he left the presidency. He had given up dancing and fox hunting, but he was still an active and vigorous man. On a typical day, he got up at dawn and inspected the progress of his workmen. Then he had breakfast, mounted his horse, and rode around the plantation. As usual, guests — a mixture of old friends, well-wishers, favor-seekers, and the merely inquisitive — abounded. At dinner, he noted, "I rarely miss seeing strange faces, come as they say, out of respect for me. Pray, would not the word curiosity answer as well?"

After the midday meal, Washington talked with his company, took a walk, and worked on his always enormous stacks of correspondence. In the evening, he drank a glass of wine punch or beer or, if old friends had come to call, champagne. He usually went to bed at nine o'clock.

Washington had spent many years looking forward to this tranquil life. Less than a year and one-half after it began, however, it was interrupted. In July 1798 Washington received an astonishing letter from President Adams. Relations between the United States and France had been deteriorating rapidly, and Adams had told Congress that the country must prepare for war. Now he informed Washington that he had reappointed him commander in chief of the American army!

As a young man, Washington had said he found the sound of bullets "charming." Since then, however, he had heard more than his share of such sounds. "My first wish," he said about war in 1785, "is to see this plague to mankind banished from the earth." Washington was anything but pleased by Adams's request that he return to military service, but as usual, he felt he could not refuse.

He was soon busy with the grinding job of putting together an army — selecting officers, conferring with heads of government departments, drafting papers, even attending military parades. In early 1799, however, war tensions eased as the Adams administration and French diplomats worked out

> *I never mean, unless some particular circumstance should compel me to do it, to possess another slave by purchase, it being among my first wishes to see some plan adopted by which slavery in this country may be abolished by law.*
> —GEORGE WASHINGTON

successful negotiations. Washington would not have to lead another army into battle.

Washington had begun to speak of the likelihood that he would not live much longer. Now he had time to write a will. The document, written in July 1799, covered 28 pages. It named Martha as the inheritor of his estate, and provided for other members of his family and friends. It also provided for the freeing, after Martha's death, of all the slaves at Mount Vernon.

Slavery was a fact of life in the world into which Washington was born. The institution was accepted without question by most of his contemporaries, but as he grew older, he became increasingly aware that it was immoral and unjust. Long before the Revolution, Washington had taken the unusual position of refusing to sell any of his slaves or to allow slave families to be separated. During the Revolution he took the even more unusual step of campaigning for the desegregation of the free blacks serving in the New England militias.

After the Revolution, Washington told an English friend that he "could clearly foresee that nothing but the rooting out of slavery can perpetuate the existence of our union." As though foretelling the

Washington discusses haying with a Mount Vernon worker. The retired president, fascinated by everything that involved his plantation, continued to make daily inspection trips on horseback. He took his last ride — in an icy rainstorm — just two days before his death in December 1799.

VIRGINIA MUSEUM

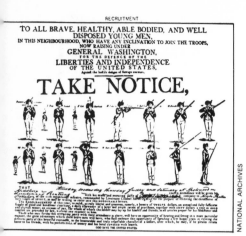

Washington ordered copies of this recruiting poster distributed in 1798. Soldiers' pay had improved since the Revolution years, when an enlisted man received $4 per month. In 1798 men were being offered a $12 bonus for joining the army and the "liberal and generous" sum of $60 for each year served.

The basis of our political systems is the right of the people to make and to alter the constitutions of government.
—GEORGE WASHINGTON

future, he said that if the South should ever separate from the North over the issue of slavery, he would "move and be of the northern" division.

Washington's will directed that, prior to their emancipation, the children of the Mount Vernon slaves "be taught to read and write, and brought up to some useful occupation." Although this provision of his will could not be followed — Virginia's laws prohibited the education of blacks — Martha heeded her husband's wishes. A year after his death, she freed her plantation's 300 slaves.

December 12, 1799, was a cold and cloudy day at Mount Vernon. An early snowfall turned to hail, then to hard, icy rain. Despite the weather, the 67-year-old Washington spent five hours on horseback, riding around his farmlands.

The next day he had a sore throat. His secretary, Tobias Lear, later wrote that his employer "took no measures to relieve it; for he was always averse to nursing himself for any slight complaint." Washington's throat got worse, and Martha sent for medical help. The primitive medical remedies of the day — most of which involved drawing off large quantities of the patient's blood — were, however, powerless to deal with the spreading infection.

Washington knew, as he said to Lear, that he "had but a very short time" left. When Lear denied that Washington was close to death, the general smiled. He said, Lear reported, "that he certainly was, and that it was the debt which we must all pay."

In severe pain, Washington never complained, but as he grew weaker, he began to worry about being buried alive. "I am just going," he told Lear. "Have me decently buried, and do not let my body be put into the vault in less than three days after I am dead." Lear nodded, unable to speak. "Do you understand me?" asked Washington. The secretary said he did, and then Washington spoke his last words: "'Tis well." It was December 14, 1799.

Four days later, Washington's body was placed in a tomb on the Mount Vernon grounds. Friends, relatives, cavalrymen, army officers, and foot soldiers accompanied the coffin as volleys of gunfire echoed through the still, cold air.

The world mourned. Flags flew at half-mast and church bells tolled in England. In France, the death of the "great father of liberty" was marked by black arm bands and emotional speeches. And from Boston to Charleston, from the Atlantic Coast to the frontier, in villages and cities all over the United States, Americans wept at the news of Washington's death.

In the nation's capital, 10,000 people watched as congressmen and government officials led a somber parade through the streets. The crowd was silent as a great white horse passed them; it carried Washington's saddle and in its stirrups were his boots, which had been turned backward to symbolize the death of its master.

Tributes to America's great leader poured in from all over the world. Among the most moving words were those of Samuel T. Coleridge. "Tranquil and firm he moved with one pace and in one path," wrote the British poet. "Among a people eminently querulous and already impregnated with the germs of discordant parties, he directed the executive power firmly and unostentatiously. He had no vain conceit of being himself at all; and did those things only which he only could do."

> *First in war, first in peace, and first in the hearts of his countrymen.*
> —HENRY LEE
> American patriot, from his eulogy of Washington

Dying at the age of 67, Washington is surrounded by doctors, relatives, and members of his household staff. When the ex-president's eyes closed for the last time, his wife said, "All is over now. . . . I shall soon follow him." Three years later, Martha Washington was buried next to her husband at their beloved Mount Vernon.

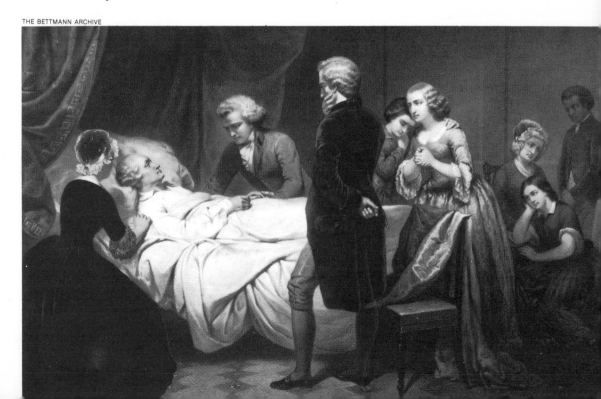

Further Reading

Burns, James MacGregor. *The Vineyard of Liberty.* New York: Vintage Books, 1983.

Cunliff, Marcus. *George Washington, Man and Monument.* New York: Little, Brown, 1958.

Emery, Noemie. *Washington: A Biography.* New York: G.P. Putnam's Sons, 1976.

Flexner, James Thomas. *George Washington, the Forge of Experience.* New York: Little, Brown, 1965.

———. *Washington: The Indispensable Man.* Boston: Little, Brown and Co., 1974.

Ketchum, Richard M., ed. *The American Heritage Book of the Revolution.* New York: American Heritage, 1958.

Knollenberg, Bernhard. *George Washington: The Virginia Period 1732–1775.* Durham: Duke University Press, 1964.

McDowell, Bart. *The Revolutionary War: America's Fight for Freedom.* Washington: National Geographic Society, 1967.

Nettels, Curtis P. *George Washington and American Independence.* New York: Little, Brown, 1951.

Rossiter, Clinton. *Seedtime of the Republic.* New York: Harcourt, 1957.

Wall, Charles Cecil. *George Washington: Citizen-Soldier.* Charlottesville: University Press of Virginia, 1980.

Chronology

Feb. 22, 1732	George Washington born in Wakefield, in the British colony of Virginia
1750	Appointed surveyor of Culpeper County, Virginia
1752	Appointed major in Virginia militia
1753	Sent to Pennsylvania to demand French withdrawal from the Ohio Valley
1754–63	French and Indian War
1755	Washington serves as aide to British General Edward Braddock during British defeat by French and Indians
1755–58	Commander in chief of Virginia's army
1758	Takes part in successful expedition against the French at Fort Duquesne
1758–75	Serves as member of the Virginia House of Burgesses
Jan. 6, 1759	Marries Martha Dandridge Custis
1765	British Parliament passes the Stamp Act
1769	Virginia burgesses protest British taxation of the American colonies
Dec. 1773	Colonists defy British taxation at the "Boston Tea Party"
1774	Washington attends First Continental Congress
1775	Elected general and commander in chief of the Continental Army
July 4, 1776	Declaration of Independence issued
1777–78	Washington survives bitter winter with troops at Valley Forge, Pennsylvania
Oct. 1781	Defeats British General Charles Cornwallis at Yorktown, Virginia, which leads to the end of the Revolutionary War
1787	Elected president of the Constitutional Convention, held in Philadelphia
June 1788	U.S. Constitution is ratified
Feb. 4, 1789	Washington is elected president of the United States
Feb. 13, 1793	Reelected president
April 22, 1793	Issues neutrality proclamation in response to growing hostilities between France and Britain
1794	Puts down "Whiskey Rebellion" in western Pennsylvania
1797	Retires to Mount Vernon
1798	Reappointed commander in chief of the U.S. Army
Dec. 14, 1799	Dies at Mount Vernon after a brief illness

Index

Roger Bruns is Director of Publications of the National Historical Publications and Records Commission in Washington, D.C. His books include *Knights of the Road: A Hobo History*, published by Methuen, Inc. He is also the author of *Thomas Jefferson* and *Abraham Lincoln* in the Chelsea House series WORLD LEADERS PAST & PRESENT.

Arthur M. Schlesinger, jr., taught history at Harvard for many years and is currently Albert Schweitzer Professor of the Humanities at City University of New York. He is the author of numerous highly praised works in American history and has twice been awarded the Pulitzer Prize. He served in the White House as special assistant to Presidents Kennedy and Johnson.